Launching Financial Grownups

Live Your Richest Life by Helping Your (Almost) Adult Kids Become Everyday Money Smart

BOBBI REBELL

WILEY

Published by John Wiley & Sons, Inc., Hoboken, New Jersey.
Published simultaneously in Canada.

For general information on our other products and services or for technical support, please contact our Customer Care Department within the United States at (800) 762-2974, outside the United States at (317) 572-3993 or fax (317) 572-4002.

Wiley also publishes its books in a variety of electronic formats. Some content that appears in print may not be available in electronic formats. For more information about Wiley products, visit our web site at www.wiley.com.

Library of Congress Cataloging- in- Publication Data

Names: Rebell, Bobbi, author.
Title: Launching financial grownups : live your richest life by helping your (almost) adult kids become everyday money smart / by Bobbi Rebell, CFP.
Description: Hoboken, New Jersey : Wiley, [2022] | Includes index.
Identifiers: LCCN 2021062800 (print) | LCCN 2021062801 (ebook) | ISBN 9781119850069 (cloth) | ISBN 9781119850083 (adobe pdf) | ISBN 9781119850076 (epub)
Subjects: LCSH: Young adults—Finance, Personal. | Teenagers—Finance, Personal. | Financial literacy.
Classification: LCC HG179 .R336 2022 (print) | LCC HG179 (ebook) | DDC 332.024084/2—dc23/eng/20220112
LC record available at https://lccn.loc.gov/2021062800
LC ebook record available at https://lccn.loc.gov/2021062801

Cover Design: Wiley
Cover Image: © ihba/Adobe Stock

SKY10032944_020122

For my father, Arthur Rebell
and in memory of my mother, Adele Rebell

Contents

Foreword

I will never forget my first television interview with the incredible Bobbi Rebell at Reuters in 2016. We were new friends, having met a few weeks earlier when she moderated a panel I was on at the 92nd Street Y in New York City. We chatted afterwards, and I remember meeting her husband, Neil, who had come to the event to support her. We all bonded over our mutual interest in making money less intimidating.

Bobbi, who was a global business news anchor at Thomson Reuters at the time, asked if I would do an interview with her about my latest project. After 15 years, I had updated my #1 New York Times bestselling book *The Automatic Millionaire*, and Bobbi wanted to amplify the critical messages this little book has taught millions. Over our talk together I highlighted the simple, yet life-changing power of paying yourself first, saving money automatically, and the importance of buying a home. Once again, we found ourselves very much in agreement as I explained my belief that there are really two primary escalators to building wealth in America – investing in stocks and in real estate – and the sooner you start investing, the easier everything in life is. Bobbi had bought her first home at age 23 and had been investing since she was a teen. But her dad worked on Wall Street, and she had a very proactive grandfather who pushed her to learn about investing at a young age. She knew she was more the exception than the rule. She also realized she had learned about investing from family, not from school.

And so Bobbi asked me, "why don't they teach this stuff in school?" I told her that was a great question. *The Automatic Millionaire* has sold over 1.5 million copies and truth be told, it shouldn't have been needed. Everything that I share in this book should have been taught in school before we reached tenth grade. The interview inevitably turned to a problem that Bobbi and I are both concerned about: The single biggest mistake we as adults make is that we don't teach our kids specific, adult, everyday and long-term money skills. Our kids become grownups and often make financial mistakes right out of the gate that can set them back for decades, often for life. Life would be easier for everyone, I said, if our schools had a mandatory financial education class that you had to pass to graduate.

After the interview, Bobbi asked me to do another interview for her syndicated personal finance column and we continued this conversation. "David," she said, "your next book should be a book about kids and money. You should write a book parents can use to teach their almost-adult children real-world money life skills because the schools aren't getting it done." I laughed, having just updated three books in a year. I was also working on finishing my thirteenth book, *The Latte Factor*.

I said, "I'm never going to write another financial book. You, my friend, should write this book!"

"Maybe I will," she said.

And then, fortunately for us all, Bobbi did.

The book you now hold in your hands, *Launching Financial Grownups*, is truly sensational and critically important if you are a parent or grandparent, or you simply have a young person in your life you care deeply about and want to help be smarter with their money. *I am very grateful Bobbi wrote this book because my family is going to use it!*

What I love about this book is that *Launching Financial Grownups* is not only about generational wealth education, but also about relationships and communication. There are fantastic books out there focused on teaching little kids basic money skills. But Bobbi is speaking to parents, grandparents, and others in older generations about young adults, ages 16 to 26. Those years are critical. We may always see our children as our precious babies, but the truth is we need to learn how to let them be their own financial grownups when they are ready. And it is our job to get them ready.

The book presents a curriculum tied to adulting milestones for which all of us need to be prepared. We owe it to our kids to get them ready for both the opportunities and the challenges that will come their way. Candidly, this book was a wake-up call for me and my family. I have two boys, ages 18 and 12. My oldest will head to college soon, and reading this book is a reminder that I have much work to do to really prepare him for the financial journey he's about to encounter, both in college and out in the "real world." I am grateful for the roadmap in this wonderfully written book. The stories and interviews Bobbi did with leading parenting and money experts, as well as psychologists and therapists, make this enjoyable, relatable, and actionable. I know it can help you educate and protect your family and give you the skills to empower the next generation.

Let's be honest. It's not easy to launch a financial grownup, and yet the benefits will be well worth the effort. This book will show you and your kids and loved ones the way. I believe if we provided our children with mandatory financial education in school, much of the financial struggles we see could be fixed. I also have come to accept that in our lifetime, financial education in school will not happen on a national level that is test-based and a part of the core curriculum.

That's where this book comes in. We are the ultimate stakeholders in our young adults' financial success. And no one is exempt. Even the kids of wealthy parents can burn through an inheritance pretty fast without the right education and guardrails. Many of us have nurtured our kids through childhood, praising every accomplishment and trying to make their lives easier because we love them more than anything. But we often don't stop and purposefully think about the life skills they will need to launch as their own independent financial grownups. Letting go is hard. But that's part of the deal when you become a parent. Don't worry – it's not too late! But the time is now.

Bobbi has provided us all with a fabulous guide to *Launching Financial Grownups*. I welcome you to this journey and I salute your efforts. You are about to do important work.

To your richest life.

David Bach
10-time New York Times bestselling author,
including *The Automatic Millionaire®*;
Smart Women Finish Rich®; Start Late, Finish Rich®;
and *The Latte Factor®*

Preface

Tuesday, May 25, 2021

This was one of the happiest days of my life.

It was not my wedding day.

It was not the day I had a child.

It was not the day I celebrated a big family milestone or career achievement.

And ironically, it was not because it was the day I signed the contract for this book, which happened as well.

The joy came in a windowless conference room in midtown Manhattan on a gray spring day, where I sat with my husband and 24-year-old stepdaughter, signing piles of very grownup documents that would make Ashley a home-owner. The event followed two years of her living at home to save money after college, including the COVID-19 pandemic when we were *all* home all the time.

Looking back, I can remember so many times I thought this day would never come. This moment did not come without many setbacks and very tough discussions. Yes, at age 24 Ashley was buying a New York City co-op apartment. Because of the particulars that apply to the Manhattan market, my husband and I had to cosign. But it wasn't our money paying for the apartment or the closing costs. Nor would we be paying anything toward the ongoing costs of home ownership. Ashley was on her own for this project, as we liked to call it.

She would now be on the hook for monthly maintenance, a mortgage, and of course the Wi-Fi bill. If the building had an assessment, it was all hers. Laundry time? She was on-duty as well. The same goes for sourcing all the things that had to go into her new home and managing a new stream of bills, including homeowners' insurance and New York City real estate taxes. We were done. She was fully aware of every expense in her new and financially independent life. She had budget projections and a good-enough emergency fund.

Earlier that day we had done a walk-through of the L-shaped studio apartment that was to become Ashley's new home. She had been saving for this dream since she was 13 years old. While my husband, Neil, Ashley, and the real estate agents went around checking that the outlets were working and the appliances were functional, I stood there watching — and tears of both happiness and terror started to flow.

I was 23 years old when I became a homeowner. Like Ashley, I lived at home after college. As a journalist, my job didn't pay as well as her consulting job does, relatively speaking, so I had temporary help from my parents, with a specific cutoff schedule. We jokingly called it an exit strategy. That early and specific push to homeownership and the financial awareness that it forced me to understand were the foundation of my future interest in finding and sharing the best ways for young adults to create their own financial lives.

There is no one path. Homeownership is just one road that can be taken to create an adult financial life separate from parents or other family who may have taken care of you up to that point. We'll talk about many other potential routes to launching financial grownups here. But I do believe most of us share a common goal: To give our children the gift of knowing they have everything they need to be financially independent of us.

One of the experts you will hear from in this book, parenting coach Allison Task, explains why a focus on finances is so essential in helping our kids mature into their grownup lives. "One of my clients said to me, 'I do not want to deprive my daughter of the opportunity to earn and pay for their first shitty car. I'm not depriving my daughter of the pride of ownership.'" Task went on to explain that the mother is wealthy and could easily buy a fancy car, like the Porsches and BMWs that are all over their neighborhood. But she had a very specific reason for not choosing to do that. "Neurologically, there's something to the pursuit and the earning and the satisfaction of that thing [Mare] Winningham talks about in *St. Elmo's Fire* (Columbia Pictures, 1985):

> Yea . . . ya wanna know what's great? Last night I woke up in the middle of the night to make myself a peanut butter and jelly sandwich . . . and ya know, it was my kitchen, it was my refrigerator, it was my apartment . . . and it was the BEST peanut butter and jelly sandwich that I have had in my entire life.

Who knew that in 2021, as I write this book, that urge to create one's own life and declare adult independence would have become so complicated – and even controversial? The coronavirus amplified a trend that has been growing. Countless adult-age children returned home to quarantine with their parents, including my own 21- and 24-year-olds.

At first this appeared to be a new complication for my mission to help parents raise financial grownups, a project I started several years ago. After all, young adults could now more easily fall back into childhood roles – and who were we to do anything but welcome them to extend their stay in our homes or return. It was a global pandemic. We wanted them safe at home: our home.

Countless millennials and Gen Zers were taking work calls and attending class on Zoom from their childhood bedrooms. Was allowance far behind? Did they expect Mom to make them a grilled cheese sandwich for lunch and do their laundry, too? How was this going to work? And how much of a detour would this be for them in establishing their own financially independent lives?

Everyone's job seemed to be at risk or already gone. Family businesses were in crisis. No one knew what the future would hold – or when the kids would move out again.

Time went on. Families, including my own, settled in. We temporarily moved out of the city to a house in upstate New York, where we expected to live for "15 days to stop the spread," as the authorities famously put it. It soon became clear that was an unrealistic timeline and we were in this for the long haul.

Our first night at the house, we sat down and had a meal together. Our 12-year-old noted that this had never happened before with all five of us.

He was right. We were always on different schedules and never thought to do anything about it. Talk about feeling like a bad parent.

Then family meals kept happening. Like many families who no longer had kids and parents coming and going from school, activities, and work, we started to really enjoy the daily ritual. We kind of liked having "the kids," around even though they were in their twenties, at home. A routine developed. My husband, stepdaughter, and I were all working. My stepson finished out his sophomore year at college virtually from his bedroom. My 12-year-old completed sixth grade via Zoom. We were all at home all the time. We were less busy. There was a lot less logistical planning and more hanging out. We weren't running late to get somewhere. There was time. We started talking more.

Some of those talks were with our older kids about our own finances, because sometimes they were in the room when things came up. We had avoided sharing much when they were younger because we did not want them to worry – or to know where we'd messed up. They had never expressed much interest. Their college tuition bills were paid, and as far as they knew we never had any stumbles. They had no idea all the ups and downs we had over the years. It became apparent that we had sheltered them too much by not giving them a realistic view into adult financial realities.

On the upside, it became clear that with so much upheaval in the world, the older kids were more willing to listen. They were hearing stories about massive job losses. They were worried and asking questions. They were paying attention to our answers. It was starting to sink in: their financial outlook was closely tied to ours.

And since they were quarantined, they had nowhere to go.

We had a captive audience.

We also started to realize that this financial dialogue was a two-way street. We were all stakeholders. The conversation was about more than teaching them financial independence from us so we could have our financial freedom. We needed our kids to know more so they could be our backstop in case the unimaginable ever happened. What if we needed them to take care of us? Living through the coronavirus pandemic created a new urgency to make sure our kids were ready for the next who knows what.

We were not alone. I started to hear stories of kids leaving school to come home and help save their parents' businesses. Many stepped up to help out with bills. Family finances tend to become a lot more transparent in a crisis. I have been so impressed with all the young adults who rose to the challenge of giving back to their parents when they needed them most.

That is the silver lining in this unique chapter of our lives. The time families are spending together has created a season of our family evolution where we have had few distractions and many opportunities to better understand each other. Families have bonded in a common mission: to protect the family financial ecosystem. It's one thing to "get financially naked" with your partner; it's another to do it with your kids no matter their age.

The door has been opened to financial conversations happening more often and more organically. It's pretty much impossible to filter conversations when you are with everyone all the time. People started to let down their guard while we were quarantined. Information leaked out. And we started to see things we used to be too busy to notice.

For my family, because we are all in the same place, all the time, the kids literally see how intensely my husband and I work. They see how our cash-flow expectations can sometimes impact our decision-making. They have a front row seat to witness tough decisions we sometimes make about how best to spend our money. They also see that we still make some mistakes along the way and that it is not always smooth sailing. They see how frustrated we get when we can't buy something because we have to allocate savings to something urgent and unexpected, like a big repair or a medical bill. They see us make tough choices about spending and how often we can go out with friends to nice dinners. They know our financial resources are not unlimited despite each of our accomplishments.

On the flip side, we have also been able to see more clearly why the kids make decisions that used to baffle us. We observe more and can better understand the context. Money conversations that used to focus on simply getting money to pay for something they want have largely gone away. When they do come up, there is a new sense of appreciation of all the work it takes for us to earn the money to give to them.

Will this progress in communication and transparency last when the world opens up again and we no longer have a captive audience? Let's hope.

For families, I see an opportunity to hit the restart button on some of the bad habits we as a society have developed that undermine our true goal: launching the next generation of financial grownups and giving all of us the best shot at the financial security and freedom that we all deserve.

Introduction

In October 2019, Kelly Ripa appeared on *The Jimmy Kimmel Show* and joked about how her son, Michael, was adjusting to being an adult: "He hates paying his own rent, and he's chronically poor. I don't think he ever really experienced extreme poverty like now."

The comment, taken by some out of context, sparked some backlash. But Ripa stood by her parenting strategy, posting later on Instagram, "Michael goes to college and is a senior and works full time. He is in his first non-parent subsidized apt with roommates. I didn't grow up privileged and neither did @instasuelos [her husband, Mark Consuelos]."

The truth is, Ripa and her husband are probably doing a better job at helping their kids become financial grownups than the majority of Americans. Data from Merrill Lynch and Age Wave shows that 79 percent of parents are providing support for their adult children.[1] As so-called helicopter parents get older, they seem to be doubling down on their overparenting. This is having a huge impact on their adult children's ability to gain financial independence. Many aging Gen X parents are on a dangerous path that could have catastrophic consequences for their own golden years. I first witnessed this phenomenon as a parent. And then, as a business journalist and a CERTIFIED FINANCIAL PLANNER™, I realized I could become part of the solution.

It started on New Year's Eve 2019.

My two older kids, both in college, had come home for the holidays. We had been discussing putting their earnings from their jobs into Roth IRAs. They would then be able to grow their money without paying taxes on the earnings. They both had agreed to do it. #parentingwin

Yet here we were, hours away from the deadline to open an account. It wasn't done. Nothing was happening. I had given them both the phone number and email of the brokerage firm we used as well as the contact

1

information for an actual human they could call with questions who had been assigned to our family. I had told them that I was available if they had any questions. And they were free to research and find their own investing platform if they didn't want to use the same company. I had reminded them of the deadline. They had said they would do it.

But here we were.

And here I was, having spent a couple of decades as a financial journalist. I actually wrote the book about becoming a "financial grownup." After the book came out, I had gone one step further to bolster my knowledge and became a CERTIFIED FINANCIAL PLANNER™ practitioner. I was facing the harsh reality that I, as a parent who knew on paper what should be getting done, could not get my own kids to do this one simple thing.

My own journey into this laser focus on getting adult kids to pay attention to their personal money situation started a few years earlier when I was a full-time business news journalist at Reuters. After 15 years in the business, I was the old guard. Younger colleagues would ask me for money advice. I always thought that was odd, because literally everything is available online. (The IRS website, irs.gov, if we are being honest, is pretty awesome. Check it out sometime.)

But the advice was never put in human terms, so it felt like a chore to them. They wanted to hear from someone they viewed as accomplished. They wanted to hear how successful people – role models – made financial decisions in the context of real life. And of these financial decisions, they wanted to know which ones were the most important for accomplishing their larger adult goals. From my experience offering guidance to my younger colleagues, I came up with the idea for my first book, *How to Be a Financial Grownup*.

In my years of journalism, one skill that had carried me far was my ability to identify and then get high-profile people to be interviewed. I always made sure they had a great experience, so they would come back. At one point, when I led booking at CNN's short-lived business news network, CNNfn, I supervised a staff that scheduled as many as 50 guests a day on various programs. I loved chatting with them before and after the segment. The guests were fascinating people with so much more to say than the three minutes typical of a television segment – often focused on data and quick tips – would allow. They had valuable life lessons to share. But a short television segment did not allow for that.

And then the big idea: What if I could give these high-profile people the opportunity to share personal money stories, not just regurgitate the data their company compiled in a survey. Now that would motivate and inspire readers to become financial grownups. I started close to home with the editor in chief of Thomson Reuters: Steve Adler. He loved the concept but was skeptical about whether I would be able to get what were effectively business "celebrities" to really share personal stories. That said, he was the first one to agree to participate, and I am forever grateful.

In the end, I pulled it off. *How to Be a Financial Grownup* featured a mix of business headliners from Tony Robbins, Kevin O'Leary, and Sallie Krawcheck to Cynthia Rowley and Jim Cramer. I even managed to snag an impromptu interview with actress and entrepreneur Drew Barrymore. I extended the concept in podcast form, and with about 350 episodes have been able to continue the conversation with young adults (and financially young adults of all ages) through that platform.

But I've also come to realize as my own children become young adults that parents play a bigger role than many of us fully appreciate. In an ideal world, my young colleagues at Reuters who were so hungry for money advice would have started their journey toward financial literacy at home.

Sometimes we, the parents, are the obstacles keeping them from truly growing into their own and moving away from dependence on us. The term *helicopter parent* grew in our culture for a reason. It's pretty accurate for many of us. If we coddle our kids financially, they will feel safe and protected. If we had a tough time in our own childhood, we want to shield them from the pain. Life is stressful enough. We want them to have an ideal, blissful, carefree childhood. But then what? How will they ever be on their own? And how will we secure our retirement if we continue to support the next generation at the expense of ourselves.

The urgency of this was becoming more apparent.

Here's the thing: if young adults don't launch as financial grownups, we, their parents, will not have the financial freedom we deserve and need as we age and move into our golden years. Without our children's independence, we risk our very survival. We pay for things for our kids with the best intentions. They are working hard. They deserve it, right? Plus, we don't want them to worry about us financially, and if we say no they might think we can't afford it and that we are in financial trouble and then panic.

Our own egos play a role. We've been trained that our #1 priority is to make our kids feel safe and secure. But in reality, our top priority should be giving our kids the skills they need – including financial skills – to survive and thrive independently from us. The coronavirus pandemic has amplified the urgency of this cultural phenomenon. In the spring of 2020 when the U.S. government began to implement stay-at-home orders, multigenerational living situations became much more common. College students were sent home from their dorms to continue learning online. Many young adults in their twenties left their roommates to shelter with their parents and sometimes grandparents. Suddenly everything we took for granted about the typical life stages of young adults was turned upside down.

With that came countless money questions. If a 20-something child came home, would they contribute financially to the household? How would that look? Many parents reported suddenly finding themselves at a loss. There was no precedent for the situation. Who pays for what? It seemed weird to charge the kids for groceries or for the Netflix account.

What if the kids were still employed but a parent was one of the millions of Americans who lost their job because of all the mandatory shutdowns? Would the child then support the parents? For how long? How would this in turn impact the next generation's ability to move forward as financially independent adults. What if there were grandparents in the mix? What would their place in the family look like from a financial perspective? How would everyone communicate and resolve expectations?

The pandemic has created a new layer of urgency to get our intergenerational money situation in order. Parents who spent more than they could afford supporting adult children may not have enough saved in an emergency fund for a rainy day – or a pandemic. They could become a financial burden on those very children, potentially creating a multigenerational downward spiral. And as we have seen with the pandemic, the economic balance can change faster than we imagine.

We may not have as much time as we think.

New data finds that nearly half of empty nester parents still financially support their adult children. And it's not just a one-time cash injection to buy a first home. The support often includes groceries, rent, cell phone bills, car payments, and dining out, according to data from 55places, an adult community comparison site.[2] According to a report by Merrill Lynch and Age Wave, 58 percent of young adults ages 18–34 say they can't afford their lifestyles without parental support. And parents who expect eternal gratitude from their children may get an unwelcome surprise as the kids get older. According to financial psychologist and CFP® certificant Brad Klontz, subsidizing adult children can backfire:

> It's not just dependence on money. It's a whole psychological syndrome. It basically leads to people who are less motivated, having less passion. They actually are more likely to sort of have self-loathing and depression, not feeling good about themselves. There's no sort of sense of purpose. And then ironically they end up resenting the source of the income.

Klontz adds that parents often use money for their own psychological reasons. They want to feel important and maintain their connection to their children. They use money and dependence as a tool to do so. Parents want to be needed.

I have seen this in my own home in recent years, as my husband and I have co-parented two children through their teens and now in their early twenties. We have interrupted vacations to help a child respond to a jury duty notice just before a deadline (call the number on the letter!) and have put off our own work to fill prescriptions and mail them to school rather than push a child to manage their own health care. We pay phone bills, give them an honor policy on charging things to our credit cards, and, yes, stretch ourselves financially to pay for their tuition so they will not have student debt.

Despite all the book knowledge I have as a CFP® and a longtime business journalist, I have realized that raising these kids to be financial grownups has been a lot harder than I ever imagined. My husband and I have discussions and make plans, but we don't always agree. Actually executing a plan has often proved impossible. Teaching a young child to put money in three jars labeled Save, Spend, and Give, as popularized by Ron Lieber in *The Opposite of Spoiled* (HarperCollins, 2015), is less complicated than teaching an adult child how to manage their life as a financial grownup. It may be a priority for us, but that doesn't mean they feel the same way. The relationship between the adult child and their parent is so different. There is a ton of psychology and relationship nuances involved on all sides.

Reality check: when my stepdaughter came to me to help with her 401(k) at her first job, she was on her way out the door to meet friends. I had nagged her enough that she had finally caved and set it up. She thought she was done because, as I instructed her, she had put in at least enough to get her full company match. She just wanted me to sign off and say, "Great job!"

She was already annoyed at me that her paycheck would be reduced by so much. But the money wasn't invested in anything, and she was about to walk out and didn't seem to care. So I was left with a real parenting dilemma. Do I:

- Say, "OK bye!" and let her deal with the consequence of the money not being invested – indefinitely?
- Say, "This isn't invested," explain that she needed to choose an investment, and try to walk her though the choices despite eye rolls and her insistence that she needs to leave?
- Say, "Bye!" and then just put her money into a low-cost index fund without telling her and plan to circle back later on to explain – which may never happen?

In the end I got her to sit briefly. If we are being honest, though, she still didn't see the difference between a fixed-income fund and a stock market index exchange–traded fund offered by the same company, almost checked the wrong box, and then didn't stay for the explanation after I fixed it. I "saved" her from not having her 401(k) invested but failed to actually teach her anything about investing at that time. I vowed to look for a time to circle back. But this example shows that even with all the knowledge and best intentions, it is complicated.

My podcast business partner and former *Money with Friends* cohost Joe Saul-Sehy has reminded me that his parents cut him off financially when he was 18. Although the lessons he learned in a few rocky years were really tough, he eventually found his way. The truth is that in previous generations that was likely more common. Saul-Sehy has been more financially supportive with his own kids, who are now in their twenties. Thanks to his discipline and teaching, they are both in strong financial positions for their age, making adult financial decisions for themselves. One even owns a rental property that he is managing.

Frankly, though, many of us Gen Xers, and to a large extent also Boomer parents, love to hover and "help." Many of us have gone from being just helicopter parents to snowplow parents, moving obstacles out of the way to clear the path and make life easier for our offspring. Concierge parenting, where we parents are standing by, on alert to solve problems, often by throwing money at them, is now emerging.

Realistically, chopping off support right after graduation isn't a plan most of us will stick to. So a surprising compromise may be the answer. On the surface, telling a kid to live at home until they can afford to live independently makes sense. Based on recent data, however, that strategy can backfire and can lead to lower occupational status. The concept: having kids live in their childhood home, with their parents taking care of them, keeps them in that life stage.

It seems counterintuitive, but the research actually supports the idea that having a child live independently, even if it means financially subsidizing that young adult's "independent" life leads to better career outcomes. The theory is that they are getting used to the daily rituals of financially independent living. Even if they are not paying 100 percent of the financial costs, they are starting to understand all the different money-related variables of life as a financial grownup. Parents can set up a gradual schedule to scale back on the support.

In my case, after living at home for about six months following college graduation and getting a few months of working at a real adult job under my belt, my parents helped me move into a brief rental and then buy my first apartment in my early twenties. I was so fortunate that I had a backstop, but the reality is that almost all my take-home pay went to housing costs and other fixed expenses. Sharing a 99-cent box of mac and cheese with a close friend most nights quickly made me aware of the costs of adult life. I pushed for promotions at work. I left for a better paying job. I watched my money very closely. I'm not sure I would have been as tuned in if I lived at home, with food always in the refrigerator and my laundry done each week.

Of course, this is not always financially viable for parents. Spouses may disagree, and every young adult is different in terms of their personality, readiness, and maturity. The key is that there has to be a phasing out of the financial support. We will get to that later in the book.

My work focuses on the money stories that drive us to find a path through the different life stages of growing up. But the focus had always been on the person doing the growing up. What I have not fully explored – and frankly solved for – is the role older generations, the parents and grandparents, need to play in the process.

Launching Financial Grownups is a call to action for parents of young adults who want the best for their kids but are beginning to realize that their *own* financial independence and financial separation from their children must become a priority as well. This will be your practical guide for how best to raise children to become financially responsible, independent young adults in our rapidly changing, increasingly competitive economy so they can create their own grownup lives.

Prerequisites

CHAPTER 1

Orientation

We want to raise independent human beings, but we do not want them to make mistakes.
—KJ Dell'Antonia, Author, *How to Be a Happier Parent*

Welcome to orientation, my friends! If you are reading this, we have a lot in common. We love our kids to death but fear we are totally blowing it when it comes to setting them up for financial independence from us.

In some cases, that fear is spot on. Many of us, myself included, are at a loss. That's what compelled me to write this book. I wanted to figure out why so many young adults are so financially tied to their parents these days – and why so many of our children don't seem to be as bothered as we, their parents, are by the situation.

Let me assure you that if you are investing your time in reading this, you are on the right track. Getting yourself informed and ready to take on this challenge is the hardest part. If you are confused by why this is so much harder for us than we think it was for our parents, join the club.

The good news is I have found and will share some answers to those questions. Some of the reasons are of our own doing. We think we just want to put up guardrails for our kids to protect them. We cringe when we are called out as "helicopter parents." But the truth is, many of us have gone past that moniker into what is being called "concierge parenting." The term, by the way, has been credited to Julia Townsend, the principal of St. Catherine's School in Waverley, Australia.[1] For our purposes, think of it as the more financial- and lifestyle-driven version of over supportive and overly involved parenting than helicopter parenting. We are at the concierge desk ready to solve problems, which often involves throwing money at the issue. More on that later.

Many of the reasons we as parents continue to be so heavily involved in our children's lives as they move into their mid-twenties have to do with huge cultural changes. Something as simple as Obamacare, which allowed kids to be on their parents' health insurance until age 26, created a new benchmark for perceived adulthood. Kids' phone bills often start coming in middle school, and many parents, myself included, don't think to turn them off as the kids move through the different stages of becoming an adult. Bills are on autopay, and we just keep paying.

Gen X parents also often have more in common with our kids. Many of us get along with our adult children better than previous generations. Thanks to technology, we have more interaction with them, are more accessible when they need us, and can be more involved in their lives. Modern cultural values and priorities have brought us closer in so many wonderful ways, as parents today are intentionally more active in their kids' lives.

All this makes the idea of pulling away from something that has become so much of our identity painful and uncomfortable for many of us. We like our kids. Equally important, our kids often like us and enjoy being around on a more regular basis. They aren't as eager to cut ties as soon as they reach each adulting milestone, like high school or college graduation. In some ways, we are heading into a multigenerational society where family members of various generations live and spend time together in a more fluid fashion. There is so much good coming from this, but it also complicates how we transition the next generation into adulthood.

I have interviewed many of the top parenting experts, financial therapists, and money experts in the world and am so excited to share their incredible observations on the trends that have been shaping parent-child financial relationships. The advice they share on how we can best navigate the changing landscape will prove invaluable to all of us as we go through this journey. However, we must also do the work and make some tough decisions. It is essential that we come to terms with the fact that becoming a financial grownup ourselves is no longer enough. We as parents and grandparents must bring the next generations with us. But the thinking on exactly how to do so has had a massive shift for a number of reasons that we will get into soon.

It is becoming more apparent that changing cultural expectations have impacted our approach as to how our kids will separate from us economically and why that has become so complicated. The COVID-19 crisis has added a new wrinkle to the trend but has also opened up new lines of communication about finances that are proving very helpful. In previous generations, kids were expected to function as adults by their late teenage years. But our current parental expectations and realities leave many bewildered. Several families I have spoken to for this book have told me, often in confidence, that their 20-something and sometimes 30-something offspring are still very much economically dependent on them. The parents are exhausted and distressed. They worry how their kids will fare if something were to happen to them. They wonder if the kids will be able to step up in a family emergency. Parents are deeply concerned about their kids but also are becoming truly scared for their own financial futures.

The COVID-19 Boomerang

The COVID-19 pandemic has further amplified this issue for many families. Adult children moved back home during what was also an economic crisis.

In some cases, they were being forced out of prolonged adolescence because their parents and/or grandparents need them to step up and care for them medically or financially – in some cases both. How prepared the younger generation was for this varied, and they often wished their parents had prepared them better for what was a shock to the system. They were forced to grow up and be financially responsible for someone other than themselves – when some had not even been fully financially responsible for themselves yet.

Some families experienced the opposite. Young adults moved home and into their childhood bedrooms and the family slid into old habits, including financial dependence. Meals were there for them, laundry was done, and life was good. Childhood perks are so much more appreciated as an adult! But after the initial adjustment period, an evolution of family roles began to happen for many families living in newly formed multigenerational living situations.

Many parents have told me adult offspring moving home was the silver lining to come out of COVID-19. Getting to know their kids as adults was wonderful, and they were happy to (temporarily) revisit their old family routines – only it was better in some ways. For the first time, they weren't competing with their kids' social plans to get them to sit down for dinner. They weren't rushing off to different events and activities. There was time. Lots of time.

What was most fascinating were the stories I heard about how the unexpected move home allowed parents insights into how well-prepared kids were to be financial grownups. It opened up opportunities to have conversations about economic realities that were not part of the parent–child relationship before, in part because everyone – parents and kids – had been totally overscheduled and overworked. Kids were in the room while their parents had open and honest discussions about financial challenges, which helped them better appreciate their parents' experiences. Likewise, parents got a better sense of how well their kids had been managing real-world money choices.

Remember, this was not the case where all the young adults were moving home for economic reasons, although that was often a big factor through no fault of their own. It wasn't about an adulting failure – financial or otherwise. They were moving home for both their and their parents' health and safety. Many families were able to leverage this season of their lives into an opportunity to build stronger financial foundations as a family. Total costs often came down because everyone was home so much. It opened up communication lines in ways that could not have come about through the normal course of events in "the before times," as we have started to call the pre-COVID period. It was a unique, unplanned experience that often presented exceptional challenges but also unexpected relationship and financial benefits.

Stepping Up as Stakeholders

As the grownup, you are ultimate stakeholder in your kids' success behind only the child themselves. In the Introduction, I shared the story that inspired the book: trying to get my kids to open up a Roth IRA before the deadline, only to be met with indifference and apathy. We often assume that kids are motivated and interested in having more money. But in many cases, especially if they have not had to worry about money, there is little incentive to take action. All their bills are paid. In fact, the bills are often never even seen. They take money for granted because they don't have skin in the game and have not been asked to contribute. The money is just there for them.

I've done dozens of interviews for this book precisely because even though I am a CFP® professional, I've struggled so much with this issue. My own kids have shown little to no interest in money at times. They have always had what they needed, and until recently my husband and I have kept them largely in the dark about our specific financial concerns. We wanted to protect them. We wanted to protect our privacy. We wanted them to feel secure. We never wanted them to know when we felt financially insecure. And frankly, sometimes we paid because we wanted those things more than they did.

A successful money manager who was a guest on my podcast confessed that he bought his kids cars as soon as they were old enough to drive even though they had not earned them. Frankly, he wasn't confident they would even take great care of them. He and his wife simply didn't want to be driving the kids around anymore. He absolutely thought the kids should have earned the money to pay for at least part of the cars, and he wanted them to pay for things like gas and insurance. At the end of the day, though, he didn't have a way to really enforce that because the kids knew the dad wanted them to have the transportation.

He's not alone. Many of us have used our financial resources to push our kids to do things that we believe will benefit them or to serve our own sense of what they "should" be doing. I know we are not the first parents to take a giant gulp and enroll our kids in lessons they want no part of.

I'm still not all that thankful my parents made me take piano lessons. They insisted, I resisted, and I still think it was a waste of money. My mom clearly felt that piano lessons were worth whatever they cost at the time.

Still, I find myself repeating the same parental behavior. If I had asked my son to earn the money to pay for his drum lessons so he would appreciate them more because he had skin in the game, guess what would have happened? He would have said no thank you and dropped the drums. It simply isn't something he values at this age.

It's Not Your Imagination: Things Have Changed

Let's start with how things actually have changed for our children and for us. I mentioned earlier that Obamacare created a perceived benchmark of 26 years old for financial separation. Before that change, there was a lot more pressure for young adults to get a job that included health care as soon as they were thrown off either their parents' or university's health insurance. For many, the change was often timed to getting out of college.

Without the need to get – let alone pay for – health insurance, young adults were more free to pursue nontraditional career paths because they did not need to work for a company that would provide health insurance. It bought them time to explore their interests, perhaps even to become entrepreneurs or independent contractors. The timing was right, as so many jobs evolved in the gig economy. There's a lot that is wonderful about how things have evolved.

As parents, we have raised our children to pursue their passions, at times regardless of actual talent or aptitude. Who are we to say that they won't be successful? Maybe we don't know what it takes to succeed in their desired field, and they really are going to make it. We encourage them to keep at it, to participate even if they don't win, to do what they love regardless of whether there is a clear economic payoff. But what happens when their passion doesn't pay the bills for the lifestyle we have led them to believe they are entitled to have? Who can blame us for stepping in to subsidize the dream we told our children to go after?

When I decided I wanted to be a journalist, it was pretty clear to me that my Wall Street investment banker dad had his doubts. He knew money made life easier and wanted the best for me. TV news was not just brutally competitive; it didn't pay well unless you really made it to the top. He was also paying for my Ivy League education. He told me he would support me financially while I did an internship in journalism the summer before my senior year – but only if it was in business news. His idea was that covering Wall Street would make me want to go work on Wall Street.

My dad was probably thinking the odds of me getting on camera as a TV anchor were pretty slim. He didn't want to be the bad guy and squash my dreams. I got myself that unpaid internship at CNN Business News and worked overnights getting to know the business from the likes of Maria Bartiromo, Stuart Varney, and Lou Dobbs. So that's pretty much how I ended up as a financial journalist: a compromise by a concerned parent trying to balance his hopes, expectations, and ambitions for his child with his desire to support her passion. Suffice it to say, his hope was that I would transition to a lucrative financial job after college graduation. Decades later, even now that I'm a CFP®, my father still asks when I'm going to get a job at an investment bank or a money management firm.

Getting back to the larger trends, in recent years student debt has exploded. That creates a huge roadblock for even the best prepared and most well-positioned new graduates to be financially independent of their parents. Students get a rude awakening when the first bill comes, and for many, cutting housing expenses by moving back home is actually the most financially astute decision for all the financial stakeholders. Remember, parents also take out loans to pay for their kids' education.

Home prices have skyrocketed, putting affordability out of reach for many young people. Wages have not kept up. And attitudes toward renting have changed. As a journalist I know data can be presented in many different ways, but there is compelling evidence that renting over buying is not always a bad financial decision, especially if your child wants flexibility with ever-changing economy and tax laws. At the very least, the idea of putting all your resources and stretching to buy a home has been put into question.

Liz Weston, CFP®, is the author of six books about money as well as a finance columnist at *Nerdwallet*. She is also the mother of an 18-year-old daughter. Weston is concerned about young adults getting into homes they won't be able to afford and remembers the 2008 housing bubble burst and the mortgage mess that followed:

It used to be the advice to stretch to buy a house because there was inflation, and inflation would inevitably raise your wages and you could afford it down the road. Well, there hasn't been wage inflation for a very long time, at least not for the majority of Americans.

The Xbox Doesn't Take Cash

Paper currency has been dethroned as the dominant everyday way we pay for things. Sure, we still use cash, but if we are being honest, for many of us, credit and debit cards, Zelle, Venmo, Apple Pay, and endless other digital payment options are our go-to means of buying and paying for stuff. The pandemic, with its emphasis on not touching anything, further amplified the cashless trend.

The rise of digital currency has made many of our lives easier. As grownups, we can track our spending more easily because the receipts can be digital, relieving us of having to keep track of those pesky paper ones. Many of us no longer sit down and manually balance our checkbooks. Digital apps break down exactly where our money is going and leave little room for us to "hide" purchases.

But there are also consequences for us and for our children. Money just flows so much more easily when it is digital. Our kids grow up seeing us swiping credit cards or even just holding our phones up to receivers to pay for groceries when we take them with us to the store – if we even go to the store now that so much of our buying is online and completely invisible to them. Things just appear in boxes at our homes. Our kids don't see any finite amount of money we have to spend. We must deliberately and very proactively show our kids the cost of things and go out of our way to discuss budgets and spending limits.

I know what you are thinking: we can still take an envelope, fill it with cash, and then walk them through a grocery trip. I think that's a great idea. Maybe I should have done it. I haven't. I'm guessing many of you have not either. My kids see that when we go to the machine, money comes out if we need cash, so they don't have as strong a sense of the fact that it is limited, no matter how many times we tell them. They often aren't interested because they are looking at their phones anyway. Money comes through Venmo or Zelle in their world. How did this happen? Why don't they feel motivated to learn more about money? Why don't they care more?

When my youngest son was little, I labeled three jars Give, Save, and Spend, as recommended by parenting expert and *New York Times* columnist Ron Lieber, author of *The Opposite of Spoiled*, who we will hear from later. When my son's savings jar filled up, we took the coins to the bank to deposit. We had to put all the coins into rolls. It took us hours. He said he found the exercise of doing the rolling "soothing" and a nice mental break. We discussed how interesting it was that you needed so many pennies to have the same buying power as a quarter and how much more work it was to roll all those pennies.

I made sure he was the one to give it to the bank teller. I made sure he showed me the total. I took photos. With his permission, I shared it on social media. We talked about what he could buy with the money if he wanted. But I'm still not sure he "got it" because it wasn't something that hit home. He didn't need cash to buy anything he wanted; it was all online, and the Xbox doesn't take pennies.

The lessons our kids first learn about money are priceless and effective for their purpose. As they go through their teen years and move into their twenties, we have to adapt and find new ways to make money lessons relevant to them as their world changes. For me, this has meant getting my now teenage son a debit card, where I can create incentives for him to earn his allowance, monitor how and where he spends his money, and teach him about saving and investing on an app. We may not like that our kids live their lives in front of little screens, but we'll get further if we meet them where they are.

Parenting expert KJ Dell'Antonia, author of *How to Be a Happier Parent* and former editor of the *New York Times* parenting column "The Motherload," uses the same debit card and app that I use, Greenlight, with her kids. "It's working really well because the kids – they do get, they do keep track of what they spend." The app allows parents to approve how and where their kids can spend money, sends a notification when a transaction takes place, and creates a digital system for spending, saving, giving, and even investing – echoing Lieber's recommendation, with the added bonus of it being on their phone, where their eyes are. Dell'Antonia says it is also more relevant to future financial grownups because it facilitates spending where spending happens: the internet. "They can use it on the internet to buy things. That was what was really hard for me for a while, figuring out how to give them responsibility because you can't get them a credit card."

Incentives Matter

Parenting expert Allison Task's stepdaughter had agreed to pay for half of her new phone. At first, there was no timeline and no consequence if she did not pay, so she simply kept putting it off and making promises that she would get to it. Then Task had an idea and wrote her a note that read, "I've made a mistake. Starting January 1, we will be charging you interest, and we'll be happy to explain how that works, but we've made a mistake." What happened next? "Oh my God," Task said. "Done in half an hour. She sent us a check for the full amount she owed us because she had recently started working at a local restaurant."

That little note enforcing what they had already agreed on, with a financial consequence, did so much to teach Task's daughter the importance of paying a loan and avoiding the consequences of nonpayment: interest. That lesson also protected her daughter from paying a higher price in the future, including having bad marks on her credit report and having to pay higher rates for loans on everything from cars to a new home.

It would have been so much easier for Task to just say, "Oh, she's working so hard and earning so little at that restaurant. Let's not bug her to pay off the phone. We aren't hurting so much for the money and she's such a good kid." And that is the point: If you are like me, you have so many regrets about things you should have stopped doing or could have done better but just have not.

It's easier not to bring it up and risk a confrontation, especially with often moody teenagers. Sometimes we go too hard on our kids, but often we take the easier path for us and smooth the way for our kids rather than have conflict. It's also easier not to bring the kids when you are shopping, even if it would help them understand why you are always complaining about the growing expense of gas, groceries, and other stuff. It is easier to buy them clothing online. But then when they see you hit "buy," do they really understand what's going on financially? Will they be ready when it's their turn?

We can all be more like Task and course correct when we see our kids aren't getting the message. It is often because we aren't *sending* the message. Once she realized this, Task was firm and reasonable and got the response she needed.

The Big Picture

Society is ever changing, and sometimes the harsh truth is that these changes will impact our children's ability to earn and have the money to pay for the life we have set them up to expect. We have the best intentions when we tell them they can be anything they want to be, but then maybe we exclude important caveats to that life if they decide to pursue their passion as a career. For example, if following their passion requires working in the gig economy, where they will not have a full-time, traditional corporate job with benefits like health insurance and retirement plans, it may never allow them the lifestyle they had growing up.

If we share our concern, there is a good chance they will say they are okay living with less. Many of our kids are honestly not as interested in material goods as we are. They can do without designer clothing and may even make peace with not updating their phones as often. That is their truth for where they are in their life.

The problem comes when they have to be financial grownups.

I remember joking (okay, also crying) years ago with my sister when my husband and I had to spend $6,000 we really didn't have to replace a septic tank in the yard of a house we were trying desperately to sell during the 2008 housing crisis. My sister had a similar high-priced expense with her home that was also not optional. We commiserated that we would never spend that kind of money on something like a designer handbag. We probably would even look down and judge someone who did (which you should not do – everyone can do what they want with their money). Now here we were, facing a very real grownup money situation, and we had no choice but to come up with the cash. It was painful, and it was not the last time I have been "forced" to pay for something I didn't ever imagine I would have to deal with as a grownup. I would complain that it wasn't "fair" that this is where our emergency savings was going. Are you nodding along with me on the "Life isn't fair" cliché?

Our kids may not want a ridiculously priced handbag or a fancy sports car, but they probably *will* need to have the money to fix the leaking septic tank or deal with whatever involuntary expense hits them when they are adults. They will need reliable income. They will need an emergency fund. As adults, they will need to know enough about budgeting to spend less than they make and not run up debt. They will need to know how to pay taxes, bills, and other expenses. They will need to understand how to read their paycheck and how to set up their company benefits. They will need to save money for retirement and to save money for life before retirement. They will need to know how to get and keep a job or a client, how to be able to buy or rent big things like cars and houses, and certainly how to buy insurance and other grownup financial products. They will need the education, financial literacy, and confidence to make tough money choices and will probably need you to be there for them when you can.

Most important, they will need to be ready-enough for the day you can't be there for them.

We need to accept that that is a good thing. As tough as it may be to hear, the ultimate mark of successful parenting is for your child to no longer *need* you. It won't mean they love you any less or want to be with you any less – but they have to be able to be okay without you.

Yes, like many of you, I am devastated at the thought of that. It's hard to let that part of parenting go. But the new relationship you will have with your child will be well worth it. We'll get through this together. Let's continue.

Review

1. Parents need to be wary of moving from helicopter parenting to concierge parenting.
2. Specific societal changes have transformed the parent–child money dynamic.
3. Parents need to maintain their authority, even with adult children.
4. Digital currency has complicated our approach.
5. Even the most nonmaterialistic kid needs to be taught to be a financial grownup.
6. Ultimately, parents' primary job is to make sure their children will be ready enough for the day we can't be there for them.

CHAPTER 2

The Family Ecosystem

A parent–child relationship is a financial relationship.

—Roy Feifer

After my first marriage ended, I found myself living with my parents, at age 30. I sold my apartment, packed up what little I got in the divorce, and moved into their extra bedroom. My childhood home in New Jersey had been sold so I was not in my childhood bedroom, but it felt oddly comforting regardless. I was devastated by the divorce and needed to be with my parents. I was so fortunate they were there for me.

My parents didn't charge me rent and didn't ask me to pay for my share of the groceries or the cable bill. Was I any less of a financial grownup? I'm not sure. I had a job, and I paid my personal bills. I didn't move into my parents' apartment because of a financial need. In fact, I had sold my apartment at a nice profit. But I'd be lying if I said I didn't feel vulnerable and insecure about my future – including my financial future. We did not discuss an exact timeline, but I always perceived living with them as short-term and transitional. I think my parents knew how wounded I was and did not want to push. In my mind I expected it to be a few months. It turned out to be more than a year. Looking back I'm so grateful that I had that emotional and financial backstop.

I share this story because it is essential that no one misunderstands the goals I am advocating for in this book. Parents can absolutely be generous, within their means, with their children – as long as they don't create a prolonged dependency. This is not about kicking out your kids. It's not about arbitrarily cutting them off before they are ready or just because they celebrate a given birthday or hit an adulting milestone. It *is* about being there to support them when they need you but knowing the difference between needs and wants – just as we talk about needs versus wants when it comes to spending money. Our goal as parents is to get them ready and able to cover their needs and then let them experience adulthood with all its ups and downs.

In the spring of 2020, countless young adults moved home to shelter in place with their parents during the pandemic, and many followed a similar pattern of moving home not because of financial need but because it just made sense given what was going on. This was a clear reminder that launching a financial grownup does not mean parents and their adult children can't be there for each other as a family in a crisis – financial or not. A family has to be an ecosystem that embraces its lifelong connections and support. Being a financial grownup does mean that our children have to be able to run their own lives and that as the younger generation moves through life, the roles and financial responsibilities will have to adapt to different life stages and challenges.

The Grownup Mindset

The most realistic mindset is to be able to adapt when your kids need you and to separate that from ongoing financial support of adult responsibilities because it is just easier to use money to solve problems and challenges. That said, there is nothing wrong with helping a child with the down payment for a home that will accelerate their path to financial independence if it does not impede your own financial goals and security. What should be avoided is paying their rent for a couple of decades! If that is happening, the child is living a lifestyle way beyond their means, and both generations need to do some serious introspection.

Creating or contributing to a college fund for a grandchild will ease the burden on young adults struggling to pay for the everyday expenses of parenting young children. That's a wonderful gift that will have a positive and priceless impact on the family. Remember, that grandchild's education will help launch them as financial grownups. And yes! You can absolutely treat your kids to a memorable family vacation, a nice dinner out, or a spa day. It's fine.

This all assumes that you can afford to do this – which is not always the case. According to a 2019 Bankrate survey, 50 percent of parents sacrifice their retirement savings to help their adult children.[1] In that case, we need to resist our desire for generosity at the expense of our own self-sufficiency in the years to come. It is not surprising that this trend continued during the pandemic in 2020. CreditCards.com found that 79 percent of parents who helped their kids financially during the pandemic did so with money they would have used for their own personal finance needs.[2] This data is alarming because parents are putting their own financial health at risk, increasing the chances that ironically they will need their kid's financial help.

Let's face it: the only thing worse than needing your adult kids to bail you out financially is probably them not being able to help because they are still not financially secure themselves. In fact, during the pandemic, many parents faced unexpected economic turmoil and were reliant on young adult children to help the family. That's why it is so important to develop a family ecosystem, where we can all aspire to be financially independent of each other but know that we are also there for each other in the seasons of life where we need each other.

The Benefits of a Strategic Boost

Jason Feifer is editor in chief of *Entrepreneur Magazine* and hosts several podcasts, including *Hush Money*. He lives in Brooklyn with his wife and kids. As a child, he says he was not materialistic. He would chide his dad for buying nice cars and was keenly aware that his family had a strong financial foundation.

I reached out to Jason after his *Hush Money* podcast cohost Nicole Lapin called him out for having recently admitted that his parents still paid his phone bill. Jason, age 39, appeared to be a fully financially independent and, frankly, incredibly successful adult. I wanted to hear more about what exactly was going on in the Feifer family ecosystem, so I asked his dad, Roy Feifer, to join us as well. Our conversation revealed a pattern of parental financial support early in Jason's career. In context, though, it was done with intention and purpose and got successful results that may not have happened otherwise. Support at the right time can be a powerful strategy if it can fit into your family ecosystem.

Jason explained that he resisted financial support early in his career even as his dentist dad would offer it. But Jason was ambitious, and when he got an offer for his dream job he was determined to make the move to New York City. "That meant that all my expenses went way up. I was 28 years old. It was 2008. I was making $50,000 at *Men's Health* and I got their blessing and encouragement." Jason also got their financial support. They subsidized his one-bedroom Manhattan apartment so he would not have to live far away from his office and face a tough commute while working long hours. He was also able to live without roommates. His parents were pretty hands-on when it came to the logistics of finding that place and making sure Jason knew all that would be involved in renting an apartment and running his financial life in New York. Some might say they were doing a little concierge parenting, but they also were steering him on a deliberate gradual path toward independence.

"I remember being very mindful every month," Jason explains. "I didn't really like asking them for the rent. They would always give it. There was never any pressure not to give it, but I wanted to be as financially independent as I could." In Jason's case, he was very motivated to pay his own rent, and while the plan was not formalized, he did gradually pay more and more of the rent each month as his financial situation improved over the next few years. He stressed to me that he might not have made the move to New York City for that dream job had it not been for his parents' support – both emotionally and financially. It was a strategic financial boost that was money well spent because the end result was a more lucrative and fulfilling career.

Jason's dad was very transparent with him about money during his childhood. Many conversations happened in the car. Jason recalled one memorable conversation in high school when his dad told him how much his dental practice brought in each year. "I remember being shocked by it at the time," he says. "Because it was a successful dental practice. And then immediately having an understanding of how much money was coming into the family versus how much was being spent."

Jason's dad Roy has continued to be open with his adult children even as they have had children of their own. "I do tell him exactly what our finances are, what our savings are, what's in the bank, and where we stand financially and my investment strategy." Roy explained why he felt so compelled to make sure his kids (Jason also has a sister) were aware of money and their family values. His own father, a postal worker, had passed away at age 49, after having not worked for years for medical reasons. At the time of his father's death, Roy was a sophomore in college at State University New York at Albany. "Dad was in charge, and he didn't discuss anything there. His motto was kids were to be seen but not heard." Roy, his brother, and mom had to fend for themselves. There were lots of money decisions to be made because "our finances were kind of limited," Roy told me.

Roy didn't want his wife and kids to be in that kind of predicament should anything happen to him. "So I brought to the marriage frankness and openness that everything can be discussed – and that included finances." Roy also stressed that his wife has been very much an equal in both the financial decision-making and in the discussions with their kids about money. Consistent messaging within the family is essential. The couple also let the children learn about their financial values by example and observation when they were growing up, even as the family became more financially successful. The Feifers lived a low-key lifestyle below their means in South Florida and had a large amount of savings. The parents didn't talk directly about a budget because the kids were already extremely careful with their spending and extremely financially conservative. They led by example, not by lecture.

The one soft spot for Roy was his love of luxury cars. And that's where the tables turned at times with both kids chiming in, urging restraint. At one point, Roy says his daughter, Jody, talked him out of buying her a Lexus, arguing it was too fancy and she would be embarrassed. You see, when it comes to family ecosystems, it's complicated. And parents should be aware that it can be very much a two-way street, especially as the kids get older and have their own distinct points of view when it comes to finances.

That's not to say the Feifers weren't aware of the fine line between productive support with an end goal and throwing money at a child without accountability. "You don't want a kid on the couch watching reality TV shows and not being proactive in securing his financial future. That's an enabler," Ron assured me. In their case, the kids were working hard and doing everything they could to build their own financial lives. So it made sense to help once they had their own future secured.

I was also struck by something very wise that Roy brought up: a parent–child relationship is a financial relationship. I had never really thought of it that way, and in our society, while few of us would openly frame it that way, it is often the case. We as parents feel societal pressure to use our financial resources on our children. And let's not forget that we may need our children to spend their financial resources on us at one point. There needs to be a family financial ecosystem of mutual support. In many cases it will mostly function as financial resources going from the older generation to the younger, but we all need to be prepared to adapt as needed and as we go through life.

Which brings us back to that phone bill and how it is that Jason, this non-materialistic, financially conservative guy still wasn't paying his own bill as he approached age 40.

In short, Jason defended his decision to let his dad keep paying his cell phone bill as part of their family plan – but not because he needs it. After way too many questions about this, it came out that it's basically become a family bonding ritual. Every month Roy sends out an email with things like who sent out the most texts and how much data each person is using. Jason always wins that one, and he blames it on his four-year-old who he says watches a lot of videos at restaurants. His mom wins for most text messages, and his dad wins for voice calls. In other words, the bill is no longer about the money; it's become a game they can play to connect. I'd say money well spent.

Review

1. Even after our young adult children have launched financially, we may want or need to selectively provide support during some of our child's adult life.
2. To be able to provide support for our children, we need to make sure we first prioritize our own financial well-being, and we need our children to understand that our financial needs will take precedence over their wants. Secure your own oxygen mask first, my friends.
3. Candid two-way conversations can help young adults better understand the financial decisions their parents face.
4. Establishing a family financial ecosystem that can adjust as time and needs change will create security. Parents should make sure kids know this might be reciprocal one day.

CHAPTER 3

Blind Spots

When parents try and control their teens or their young adults, they're really conveying that they don't have confidence in their son and daughter to manage their own affairs.
        —Mary Dell Harrington, *"Grown and Flown"*

The fact is, pretty much all of us have financial blind spots and make bad financial decisions at some time in our life. We often don't fully acknowledge them until well past the time they happen. But coming to terms with our own shortcomings when it comes to our relationship with money is essential if we are going to launch our kids and raise financial grownups.

I distinctly remember taking out a home equity loan to fund a summer share in the Hamptons in my early twenties. I felt very adult because I had recently bought a small co-op apartment. Not only did I consider myself fully financially independent because of this (even though I had lived comfortably subsidized at my parents' home after graduating college and had a lot of unofficial "soft" parental support), but I was also delighted to find out I now qualified to take out that home equity loan because I owned my apartment.

Happily into debt I went.

Knowing what I know now, I would be mortified if my kids went into debt to essentially go on vacation by being part of a summer share house. Buying a home was my choice, and I was voluntarily cash poor because of it. My best friend and I, who had also bought her apartment, took pride in our 99-cent Kraft mac and cheese meals. I knew my home-related expenses meant I would have to make some spending sacrifices. Specifically, I knew that with my home-related bills, this added expense of a summer share house in the Hamptons wasn't within my means, but that did not stop me from desperately wanting to be with my friends – who did not have the financial responsibilities of home ownership at such a young age. But that very grownup expense of owning my own apartment had been my choice. I could have lived at home. I could have lived with a gaggle of roommates. I chose to buy that apartment and take on the financial responsibility that came with it. But I wasn't ready to come to terms with having to say no or find other ways to pay for things I wanted at age 23. And no, I did not ask my parents advice – another decision I'm not proud of as I look back.

As we get older, hopefully we get better and more tuned into our financial decisions. Sometimes we don't, even though the stakes get higher. In many cases, including my own, we continue to make mistakes despite our added life experience. We hope the kids don't notice. Truthfully though, it's probably not that bad if they do see our missteps and learn from them.

Stop Blaming the Kids for Your Money Mess

Financial therapist Amanda Clayman has found that parents often use their children and the financial support they provide to them as young adults as an excuse for their own lack of financial stability and failure to reach their own financial goals.

They have paid for all the things they felt as parents they should provide for their kids to the detriment of their own financial preparation for the future. In many cases we as parents feel we have no choice, but we need to hold ourselves accountable for our own decisions. Remember, we're the grown-ups, and we need to own it when we make bad choices. One reason parents often spend money on child-related expenses for their teen and young adult kids, according to Clayman, is that money can often fix short-term problems or obstacles. It makes life easier for them, and makes the parents feel needed and useful. Why not pay the kids parking ticket for them, especially when the incident was an innocent mistake anyone could have made? Why not pay for their insurance for a little longer? And then of course there are the never-ending phone bills as we saw with the Feifer family. Stopping payments would be breaking a connection to the kids that parents may want to keep.

Clayman explains that parents come to her saying, "I'm in trouble, but it's not because of something like my own inadequacy here or lack of preparation or bad things that have happened for me. It's because I'm doing this selfless thing, which is helping to support and financially nurture/enable my adult child." The choice to help a child is the parents' own money mistake if it damages their own financial future. It is not selfless if creates financial hardship or other consequences for them and for their children later in life. Parents have a hard time saying no. They also have a hard time resisting the urge to help make their child's lives easier – especially if it involves a simple financial gift. And many parents offer to help without even being asked.

Jean Chatzky, CEO of HerMoney.com, host of the *Her Money* podcast, and the mom and stepmom of four young adults remembers her 24-year-old daughter signing up for some pricey Zoom workout classes during the pandemic. Although the classes were expensive, her daughter proudly told Jean she had negotiated a great deal. Chatzky remembers thinking, "That is so great. I'll pay for that. And I had to bite my tongue because she's not asking me to pay for it." Jean was well-intentioned on many levels, but had she stepped in to pay for the classes she would have been trying to solve a problem that didn't exist. Remember, her daughter did not ask for her mother to pay for the classes. Quite the opposite: she had negotiated well, knowing she would have to pay for the classes. She was proudly telling her mom about her own financial grownup moment.

That doesn't mean Jean wasn't tempted to do some concierge parenting. "She could save that money, or it would be great for her next down payment for her next apartment or whatever. But part of her being an adult is managing her own budget and making these kinds of decisions and choices. And so I need to back off."

Letting our children enjoy the feeling of accomplishment they will get by paying for things they want with money they earn is a gift we need to let them have. For Jean, affordability was not an issue. While that is not always the case, it does not stop many parents from swooping in to help their kids even when they are not asked. Clayman points out, "If a parent already has a narrative of 'I sacrifice for my children, it's what I do. It's part of what makes me a good person and a good parent, and I feel good about myself,' that can be a real source of identity and strength for a person." In the moment, we believe we can afford to solve our kids' problems and make their life more comfortable because we feel we have the cash on hand. We don't want them to think we aren't there for them. We also don't want them to think we have money problems or concerns of our own. But for any parent with a finite amount of money, over the long term, those choices are also eating into our investments and retirement funds.

A recent study by OnePoll in Britain of 1,000 parents with children who have left home found that 75 percent continued to provide financial support for their children after they have flown the nest.[1] In and of itself, there's nothing wrong with some help, especially during something like a time of transition or an expected crisis or support that helps grandchildren. Nothing magical happens at a specific day where parents need to just "cut them off." Here's the red flag, though: Of those that gave their adult children financial support, 36 percent admitted that it had impacted their own financial situation.[2] For one in ten people, that meant delaying their retirement. Ditto for having to get a second job. And 44 percent felt that when it came to helping their children, they felt they had no choice. Even more alarming, 66 percent said they dipped into their own savings, and 15 percent racked up credit card bills to help their adult children.

Parenting expert and life coach Allison Task points out that we are not only hurting ourselves financially but also depriving our kids. "You're hurting their growth. They need to fly on their own. You are literally clipping their wings because you're being selfish because you enjoy giving. So they're not having the opportunity to learn how to walk on their own."

When our daughter Ashley's first mortgage payment on her new apartment came due, part of me feared she might waver in her determination to be financially separate from us. What would we do if she asked for our help? We could not possibly let her miss a mortgage payment. Not only did she pay the bill; she also was positively glowing as she told us how excited she was to pay it herself. She was genuinely so pleased with herself for having budgeted and tracked her money well in advance so there was no question she was able to pay that bill on time now and in the future. Let me tell you, the satisfaction of seeing her joy in not needing our money was priceless.

~~Student~~ Parent Loans

Given all the talk about the student debt crisis, many of you would be surprised to know that it is very much a *parent* debt crisis. According to the Urban Institute,[3] Parent PLUS loan debt increased 42 percent in the decade ending in 2018. According to federal data cited by NerdWallet,[4] total parent debt is over $103 billion in 2021, with more than 3.6 million borrowers. We hear a lot about students having a hard time getting started in their life when they graduate with a heavy debt load. But let's not be blind to the fact that parents who take on a heavy debt load in midlife also have an impending crisis. How are they going to retire if they are servicing debt tied to their child's education?

A dear friend of mine, Nina (not her real name) confided in me that in her mid-forties she discovered her dad had been paying her student loans for two decades. She had some loans of her own and paid them off years ago. She had no idea her dad had taken on debt for herself and her siblings. He never said a word and never complained. He just quietly paid. Her guess was that he felt he owed it to her. He didn't want her to worry or to have so much debt that it impeded her ability to start her own adult life. But the truth is that had he been more transparent with her, Nina would have stepped in to pay them off once she had the means.

Look in the Mirror

Parents also tend to avoid teaching their children about money because they don't think they are qualified. They hope the schools will do it. They assume their kids will figure it out. But one of the biggest mistakes a parent can make is letting this slip through the cracks because of their own discomfort. You are the ultimate stakeholder in your child's life – not the school and the employees who work there. The question of course is how to get started. One important step is to look in the mirror at your own early in life financial mistakes and regrets and share them with your kids. We all tend to think we are the only ones who messed up early in life (and in midlife if we are being honest!), but that is ridiculous.

Liz Weston may have gone on to a career as a money expert, but she came clean to her teenage daughter about the money mess she created when she bought retirement property – in an area of Alaska with no roads – at age 26. She was dating a cop and living in Anchorage. She expected to marry him and spend her life up there. Her boyfriend had a cabin 80 miles away from the city and far from any road. "I thought that when you were retired, you would want to be in a flying-only location. So I bought 14 acres, which I still have because I literally cannot give it away."

Doing the Work

I reached out to Mary Dell Harrington, one of the leaders of the incredible Grown and Flown Facebook community of more than 200,000 parents of young adults. While she conceded that like all of us parents, there were things she might have done differently, she has successfully launched two young adults, now ages 25 and 30. Harrington was clear that this success is not something that just happens. We have to work at it.

It is a good reminder to those of us who keep hoping the kids will figure it out. They might. But do we really want to take that chance and risk the consequences to their financial future and ours? The first step is recognizing that we must give them space to learn without a lecture. "I think that there's a confusion between what is helpful about an involved parent and what can be damaging," says Harrington. "When parents try and control their teens or their young adults, they're really conveying that they don't have confidence in their son and daughter to manage their own affairs. And that's really a terrible thing."

For example, if you do give them money, take a step back from trying to stay in charge of it all. Release control. Let them make their own choices, some of which you will not like. Some will be mistakes in your mind – but they might not be mistakes for where they are in their life. They may not be mistakes at all. My friend Jennifer Barrett, author of *Think Like a Bread-winner* (Penguin, 2021), watched in horror as her teenager bought virtual merch in an online game. He then turned around and sold them to other gamers – at a profit. She was frustrated because she thought the concept of paying real-world money for fake-world things was terrible. But she also had to do a mind shift and realize that virtual or not, her child knew the market and was able to make a profitable trade.

For many Gen X parents, the urge to be so protective of our kids when it comes to money is often a reaction to the laissez-faire parenting so many of us, including Harrington, experienced: "I had a very traditional upbringing with a dad who worked and a mom that stayed at home, and I don't ever recall really talking about money with them. So that influenced my child-raising attitude." She also reminds us that some very specific things have changed for our generation, driven by technology and the infinite availability of information. Communication between generations is easier to facilitate – no more going off to college and having one phone call a week at the public phone down the hall or a stream of back-and-forth letters. We can chat and text in real time and can be available for support on even the smallest stuff. We can also send them money instantly.

Let's also not forget that the internet and droves of personal information on there have also made our finances nearly impossible to keep hidden. Home values, and exactly what we paid for our home, are easily found. Many salaries are posted online, as are some donations and other data points in our financial lives. With not too much effort, our children can have a very clear picture of our finances.

Harrington's advice to parents looking to open the conversation is to focus on money values, for example, to save for things that are important to you, such as experiences over physical gifts. She also cautions that we can't expect our children to just absorb these things as they go through their daily lives; we have to be more deliberate in the conversations we have. They can get the information, but we have to provide the context.

Harrington recommends taking the opportunity to talk to kids about money when they first start earning it, often at summer jobs. "Parents whose kids have had summer jobs or who have contributed significantly to their own college education, I think have had to sort of learn those financial literacy lessons much earlier in life – to their benefit. People talk about how much should their kids contribute family budgets right now, if they're living at home."

COVID-19 complicated this situation but also brought to light the delicate balancing act that parents and kids have to figure out as kids move into young adulthood. Parents can let kids live at home "for free," but the relationship should be recognized as completely different from when they were young children. Young adults who moved home during the pandemic often enjoyed the perks of being with their parents: saving on housing costs, free food and laundry service, possibly child care, and so on. But as time went on, the new living situations also created opportunities to have candid conversations about the financial futures of these young adults.

It also opened the door for more candid conversations between the generations about the parents and possibly grandparents' financial histories, current status, and future plans. Many parents I spoke with were able to more comfortably talk to their young adult children who moved home during the pandemic in ways they could not beforehand simply because of proximity. They were able to share with their kids their concerns about their future finances. Young adults could overhear discussions between their parents and older relatives about money and get a clearer picture of the challenges – and wins – that their parents were experiencing.

Getting Real about Our Blind Spots

I was also able to tap into the Grown and Flown Facebook community to get some insights from parents of young adults on their own money regrets, lessons and wins from their young adult years, and take on how they are applying those experiences to parenting their young adults. Here are some highlights of their responses.

> Money mistake . . . buy NEW cars when used cars would've been much less expensive! Saving cash to pay for said cars is something that I now insist for my kids to do. I will try my best to not have another car payment (life happens, so it's always a possibility).
>
> —Wendy Mast

> I trusted my ex as I was a stay-at-home mom that relied on his income and once he left I was left to still rely on him (which gave my ex control even after he left). My girls all watched my mistake and have made sure they held their own from day one. 3 out of 4 saved up and were able to purchase homes by 19 and are thriving. My other daughter is a recent college grad that is out on her own as well in an apartment with her boyfriend and they hope to buy next year.
>
> —Carin Kimmel Baldwin

> Purchasing 1st house. Family pressure to purchase. What (the) bank thinks you can afford vs what you can realistically afford. House poor. Could barely make mortgage and monthly bills. Nothing left for emergencies. No money to furnish house and initial necessities.
>
> —Karen Bellessa

> We didn't buy our first house until we had one year of living expenses saved. A couple of months later my husband lost his job, we had a new baby (I was on mat leave and had quit my job) and a decent part of our mortgage was subsidized through a special program through his job so our payment went up significantly. It was rough but thankfully we were not house poor and got through it financially due to the large amount we had saved.
>
> —Anonymous

1) Going in Debt to Start a Business that Failed. Hard Lesson Learned when the business is bust and you still must pay the Payments.

2) Running Up Credit Card Debt, Student loans and a Car Loan.

3) Always honest about our past mistakes and why we encourage them to take a different path. However, I've learned they also have to make their own mistakes.

4) We are transparent about our debt and trying to pay for things as we go to show them it's possible. We are just starting to be transparent about investing.

—Rhonda Melton Faulkner

Very transparent when they ask – I think it's good for them to know how much things cost, how much we have earned at various stages of life, what brings money stress and how to keep it at bay ie. through detailed financial tracking and budgeting. I don't want money to be a taboo topic within the family like it was for prior generations.

—Tammy Spector Li

For me, I was horribly irresponsible with money as a young adult. My parents never taught me the basics, so I was undisciplined with no thought of future planning. I tell my kids this all the time. I talk to them about the steps it took to repair my credit and what a burden that was for their father (my husband) when we got married and wanted to buy a house. It was embarrassing and unnecessary.

We taught our kids to save, talk endlessly about wants vs needs and teach by example. We have said "no" a lot over the years, but we know it will help our kids in the long run. And as a side note, be real about your strengths and weaknesses. If you know you tend to be impulsive with money, marry someone who is more frugal or have a plan if you are both spenders. My husband has turned me around and I am so thankful for his parents and what they taught him growing up.

I think kids today struggle with never holding cash, Venmo, scanning checks for deposit, debit cards and never seeing the inside of a bank or a bank statement, make it all seem fluid and easy to lose track of how much you are spending.

—Maureen Cooney Stiles

I really wish I had more info about investing at a young age. The advice I got from my dad was – always put money from your paycheck into retirement . . . and I did do that, but nothing about investing any other way . . . and no internet back then so harder to stumble upon infor-mation. I am trying to correct this with my kids and encourage them to invest even before they have a full-time job. Currently this summer we are discussing putting money in an invested Roth vs paying down their federal student loans while in school, because over time the compounded interest from investment will outweigh the below 3–4% student loan interest.

We are very open with our kids about income, finances and how we choose to spend, save. We talk about things like making credit cards work for you – card with rewards . . . pay off every month = reaping thousands of $$$ over time.

—Jenni Mouer

My parents never taught me about anything money related growing up, but I was fortunate enough to have my first employer take me under her wing and teach me financial literacy. She taught me how to balance a checkbook, establish credit and not spend beyond my means. Because of those early lessons, I avoided the pitfalls of debt and established a decent nest egg. My late husband and I did the same with our kids. We have been very open with them about finances and have been teaching them along the way. We were very open with them, and they knew we had no debt other than the mortgage on our home which we owed very little. They saw us meet with our financial planner. We discussed retirement accounts, savings accounts and how much percentage wise should be allocated to each. We taught them not to carry a balance on a credit card. My husband passed away suddenly when my kids were 15 and 13 and, as hard as that time was, we weren't left in financial ruin even though we lost the primary income earner in our family. I was able to reassure them we were going to be ok and wouldn't have to make drastic changes to our lifestyle. I sat them down and showed them all of the household bills so they would see what we were spending and how I'm managing our budget with my income alone. It also brought up a good conversation on the importance of having your paperwork/affairs in order (ie will, advanced, directives, power of attorney and life insurance). All of that is part of learning financial literacy, in my opinion.

—Ellen Crummy

Which stories do you relate to the most? The truth is that it is very complicated, and many of the situations the women in this group were kind enough to share are more common than many of us want to admit. Many of us were simply not taught about money from our parents. We were often told, or it was inferred, that specific financial milestones indicated we were adults – for example, buying the home that the bank said we could afford.

As you will see later in this book, I am generally an advocate for home own-ership. But I do not advocate buying a home that will hurt your ability (or your kid's ability) to live a financially comfortable life, as is the case if you stretch too much to buy a home that you really can't afford. The bigger red flag is when a young adult buys a home or makes another large purchase merely because it is a traditional milestone of adulting. That can be a new car that is out of their budget and requires taking on debt or simply living a lifestyle that is not yet in their financial comfort zone.

Be Their Coach, not Their Teammate

I often hear parents saying they want to be friends with their adult kids as they grow up. That may work in some areas of their life, but when it comes to financial matters a little authority and distance can be helpful. I prefer the term *coach* rather than *teacher* because it implies a drive to win, not just to impart lessons – although that is of course also part of our role as parents.

Please resist the urge to remove yourself from the situation because you don't believe you are a financial expert. You have lived your life, and espe-cially if you have made mistakes, you have a lot to teach them. For example, Harrington points out that many young people come to their parents for advice about things like negotiations – everything from rent to a salary for a job. Odds are you've rented an apartment many more times than they have. You've negotiated salary or prices on something you were buying. What if you aren't very good at it? Sharing your missteps and regrets can be just as valuable, and in some cases more valuable than your wins.

It will also humanize you and help them let their guard down. "I think there is actually a huge benefit to parents talking about things that they have done wrong and mistakes that they have made. I think in many cases, kids grow up thinking that their parents are almost super humans, that they've never made a mistake. They've never stumbled. They've never screwed up. And I think that puts a lot of pressure on kids because everybody makes mistakes," says Harrington.

We may not be consciously aware of it but as parents most of us do want our kids to look up to us and to see us as successful. Who doesn't want an A+ in parenting? But trying to maintain a perception of perfection as our kids enter the real world can become exhausting for us, and detrimental to helping our kids understand some of the financial realities and responsibili-ties of adult life.

Most of us have had friends or family that we thought had the perfect life, only to discover cracks beneath the surface. Seeing that we're not alone in our money struggles is comforting. By showing our kids a more complete picture of our financial experiences, we can take some of the pressure off them to live up to lifestyle expectations that may not be in their best interest.

Which brings us to one of the biggest stumbling blocks for our young adults: Debt. It's not all bad, which is why we need to do more than throw up red flags. More on that as we move into the Core Curriculum.

Review

1. Don't let blind spots stop you. You are the ultimate stakeholder in your child's financial future, so step up.
2. Recognize your own early adult setbacks, and share them with your kids.
3. Let the kids learn without a lecture.
4. Listen to their concerns, but resist offering to solve their problems.
5. Resist the urge to avoid talking about money because of your own perceived shortcomings.

Core Curriculum

CHAPTER 4

D Is for Debt

I paid it off last year on the day I got nominated for my second Golden Globe.

—Actor Gina Rodriguez to Stephen Colbert
on paying off her debt from the NYU Tisch School of the
Arts 11 years after graduating.[1]

What comes before F as in failure? D, as in debt. The urgent phrasing is no accident here. No parent wants their kids to feel the weight of debt. Debt will stress them out and keep them up at night. And for most young adults the true pain of debt is that it will quite literally create a road-block to the adulting milestones they are looking forward to and potentially keep them from achieving their dreams.

Debt can keep our kids from choosing the best long-term career. It can deter them from going to graduate school, because that often racks up even more debt. It can stand in the way of buying a car or a first home. Debt is often cited as a reason to delay marriage and having kids. Debt takes away freedom and if not tackled correctly can become a trigger for depression and derail so many hopes and dreams. Debt can keep them from having the freedom to enjoy life as a young, healthy adult. But let's not forget that debt is an important tool that can power so much good. Millions of kids would not have the opportunity to get a college education if there weren't loans and financial aid available. Countless homeowners would never be able to buy their own homes were it not for mortgages. Without a car loan many people would not be able to buy cars – and those cars often take them to jobs where they earn money to support themselves and their families. Our society's economy, like it or not, is tied to debt.

Many families make the mistake of simply saying to kids: Don't even have debt. That's a great aspiration. But for most of us, it is not realistic. For example, if young people don't have credit cards, it will negatively impact their ability to build a credit score. So we need to make our peace with debt and prioritize educating our kids on using various kinds of debt for good and minimizing the bad.

Jean Chatzky, as the parent and stepparent of four young adults, prioritized teaching them the best ways to use credit and why just avoiding it all together was not a realistic choice in our current culture. "It's not fun being looked at as a number but get used to it because people look at you that way. And if you want to rent an apartment and if you want to finance a car, and if you apply for certain jobs where you have to handle money, they may look at your credit score." Chatzky has talked to her kids about credit scores and how they are determined. But it is important that she also went beyond talking and gave her kids real-world experience. She made them authorized users on her cards to get them started. This is something we have done in our family as well.

Many of the key pieces of advice Chatzky had for her kids, that we should learn from, have to do with dispelling some of the myths and assumptions our young adults might make. For example, at first glance it would be logical that if you are given a spending limit by the credit card issuer of $1,000 you should not go beyond that limit. Well, that is true. But we as parents should also explain, to have the best credit score they should ideally charge only up to 30 percent of that limit. We can explain to our kids that when their credit score is calculated, the credit agencies focus a lot on something called utilization, which is the percentage of debt you owe relative to your limit. A utilization rate around 30 or below is considered excellent and will help with their credit score. In other words, they want you to have wiggle room in there.

Another common mistake young people make when they get their credit card bill is to pay the minimum amount. This is in part because the credit card companies often highlight that amount, so it appears that is the amount due. We need to make sure our children understand they should pay the entire bill on time every month. We should also let them know how important it is to pay every bill – but especially a credit card bill – on time. That is the number one factor in their credit score. One late payment can wreak havoc. It's better to pay less than the full amount than to miss a payment.

It is also important to make sure your kids know how the world of credit is evolving, so they can go in with open eyes and not be tempted to get in over their head just because they are offered financing. Here's an extreme example: Buy Now, Pay Later is a big trend right now. At first glance these seem like they are always a bad idea. There are many times when they are. We absolutely do not want to tell young adults it's okay to buy something discretionary that they can't afford because, well, most of the payments won't be due for a while. That's just borrowing quite literally from the future. It's a bad idea and should be discouraged. But when someone is going to make a purchase anyway, it is better to have a few zero-interest payments than to charge on a credit card and immediately pay interest. This is the lesser of two evils. The key is to stay in control and pay it off without incurring any interest or fees. That takes education and discipline that we as parents need to instill in our children. This isn't something you use on an impulse item. It's for responsible spending and cash flow management that they must be very much in control of when you sign up for these types of offers.

I used the concept of a zero-interest payment plan years ago when I was faced with extremely high bills from an orthodontist for our three kids at the same time. The treatment he was recommending would be most effective if it was started at younger ages: in other words, right away. But I simply could not even come close to writing a check for anywhere near the full amount of the multiyear plan, which apparently was the standard first offer when it came to this kind of thing. I decided to ask if we could spread the payments out over a few years (yes, they were that big!), and to my total surprise, only then was it revealed that they were more than happy to put us on a zero-interest payment plan so we could get the kids started at the optimal time. The fact that they were so accommodating and had a system in place seemed to tell me that this is something no one really talks about but is quite common. There is no shame in asking for a payment plan!

I remember doing a story in my days as a business journalist about payday loans. This is when someone borrows money, often at an extremely high rate, often for literally a few days. On a percentage basis the amount they charge is over the top and a horrible deal. The rates are sky high and prey on the desperation of the borrowers. Payday loans are something everyone should do their best to avoid needing. The story was originally going to expose the lenders as 100 percent villains. But the sad truth is, if someone is in that dire a predicament, it is sometimes better to pay a bill on time – the rent or the electric bill or maybe an insurance bill – than to have a huge fine and the risk of it hitting their credit score or worse. The problem is that often what should be a one-time only tool can quickly become a habit.

I realize that by even mentioning payday loans as something to talk to your kids about could get me a ton of criticism. But the risk is that our kids will feel ashamed if they are in financial trouble and seek out short-term solutions that can spiral out of control like these without letting us know. *We never want them to make bad financial decisions to avoid disappointing us.* The solution is to make sure our kids have their eyes wide open, so they know their options, the tools to use, and the ways to hopefully avoid having to deal with any of this at all.

Now let's start with the mother of all debts: student loans.

Priceless Education Is Expensive

Right now, we as a society are having a lot of healthy discussions about the value of higher education. For years, a four-year college degree has been considered one of the best ways to guarantee a young adult the ability to earn a solid living and move up economically in society. Entire industries have been built to sell parents and their teenage kids on the priceless value of a college education. Unfortunately, while we can't pin down exactly how much our individual child will benefit from a traditional four-year college, we can do some price exploration.

According to U.S. News & World Report, for the 2020–2021 school year, the average public school tuition for in-state students was over $10,000.[2] For out of state, you can more than double that number. The average private school four-year college degree in 2021 was over $35,000, with top-tier schools like Yale getting close to $60,000 for tuition alone. As the parent of a student at NYU, I can tell you the sticker shock is real.

New York Times money columnist Ron Lieber and author of *What to Pay for College* suggests starting the conversation early and letting your children know that you are saving for their education. This can start as early as middle school with showing them a 529 statement every quarter so it is clear you are planning and that they should be thinking ahead as well. Here is a sample script for parents from Lieber:

"I just want to remind you that we're saving for you to go to college. We expect you to go, if it's something that you decide is worthwhile for you, and that we decided is worthwhile for you. And we want you to know that, at this point we've got 22% of the total saved . . . and we feel really good about it, and we're making a plan and we want you to know that."

Lieber's idea is that this will help you avoid sitting down with your child at age 16 for the first time to talk about college and your expectations.

Grown and Flown's Mary Dell Harrington echoes this sentiment: "Every spring we get so many people in our Facebook group saying my heart is breaking. My daughter got into her dream school, and we can't afford it. And I just can't bear telling her that, well, probably that dream school should have never been on the list to begin with."

College Financial Aid: Make It about Them

When it comes to borrowing money for college, the ideal scenario is that you just don't. Your best bet is to tap into as many financial aid resources and other sources as you can that don't require money being paid back, in other words, scholarships, grants, and, yes, the money you have put aside for college in a 529 or other savings vehicle. And, yes, if grandparents are financially secure and want to gift tuition money to their grandchild or fund a 529, by all means accept it – with a big thank-you from you and from their grandchild.

Don't forget that college is not one lump-sum payment. It is spread out over about four years in most cases. That means you can use money you are earning along the way to supplement savings rather than take out loans. Most colleges also have simple and extremely low-cost payment plans that allow you to spread each semester's tuition over a number of payments without paying any interest or penalties. I know because my family has used those plans.

Lieber cautions parents to be very careful in taking out loans in their own names. He sees parents "borrow to the sky to make this happen" without their kids borrowing a cent. They don't want their kids to know they simply don't have the money to pay for college without debt, and they don't want to let them down. "I want people out of the shame business," says Lieber. "It doesn't do anybody any good to beat themselves up, and your kids can sense more than you know. There's a reasonable chance that they're reading your mail or peeking over your shoulder or have found some way to look at your investment accounts, or they overhear somewhat tense conversations you might be having with a spouse or with an ex, or with a financial planner or a friend." In other words, make the cost of college about their financial future, not yours. Liz Weston of Nerd-wallet agrees: "I've seen parents with massive amounts of student loan debt that they could not afford, that they're going to be paying for the rest of their lives. And that's what's scary."

Attorney Leslie Tayne and her husband currently have five kids in college. She was adamant they have skin in the game. "I had them take loans for college so that they would understand the loan process," she says. "All of them have federal loans; some have private loans. They all understand the repayment process. They understand the FASFA [Free Application for Federal Student Aid] part of it. They understand the consequence and what that means and how it impacts their credit."

The message was not always well-received. "One of my kids said, 'Why can't you just sell the house in Florida and pay for my college?'" She adds that while they were growing up, she provided for her three kids generously as a single parent. She paid for sleepaway camp and teen tours. They wanted for nothing. They were privileged. She is adamant that now that they are young adults, no matter how much money she has, her children have to step up.

Tayne tells me that in her practice she has clients who come to her weighed down with Parent PLUS loans. These are loans that parents can take out to pay for their kids' education, separate from the child's student loans. They don't have the same limitations, protections, and forgiveness options as many student loans. For example, they don't have income requirements, and credit standards are relaxed and more expensive than student loans. According to 2021 College Scorecard data, the median parent PLUS loan is $29,945.[3]

Tayne recalled a recent case where somebody's ex-spouse was suing them to prevent the other parent from taking out loans to pay for school.

When Tayne's daughter was accepted at a state school and chose to go to a very expensive private school, she was clear that the student loans were her daughter's financial responsibility. "She had accountability and responsibility for the tuition along with her federal student loans that she's completely aware of. We looked at the balance recently, and she talked to me about budgeting and how she's going to budget to try to pay that when the time comes and she's finished with school."

Harrington stresses the need to be transparent with your kids about your own ability to pay for their dream college and what they will have to pay. "I think it's important that you enlist your teen and college student's involvement in knowing that finances are tight. They cannot look at any school. If they're applying to colleges, there are certain rules about schools that they can and can't apply to, how far away they can go to school, or maybe they have to live at home." She adds that it is really important for parents to be transparent around what the financial constraints are. Many parents resist this both because they feel it is not any of their kid's business and also because they may feel some shame about not being in a stronger financial position after so many years of working.

The truth is that with so much information available on the internet, there's a good chance your kids can get information about your finances without too much effort. There's also a good chance that information will only be one piece of your financial pie and could give them a skewed sense of your financial well-being. In the end it's better to get ahead of the situation and make sure they have the correct information and as complete a picture of your financial situation as you feel comfortable giving to them.

For most families, filling out the FAFSA will reveal pretty much all your financial secrets anyway. So it makes sense to share information well ahead of time so that you, their parent, can present the information in a way in which you are most comfortable, or at least less uncomfortable.

Pamela Capalad is a CERTIFIED FINANCIAL PLANNER™ professional, Accredited Financial Counselor™, and the founder of Brunch & Budget. "I remember when I had to ask my parents for their tax return and my mom was like, 'Excuse me?' They're gonna find out eventually. You don't want them to find out at 17 when they have to fill out the FAFSA for the first time."

Proactively bringing up your situation also opens up a conversation about choices you made and why. They will benefit from hearing why you donate or don't donate to certain causes, why you invest in certain industries, and possibly some hidden expenses you've taken on that they would never know about, such as supporting a friend or relative in need. You don't have to reveal the details including who that person is, but in the spirit of the family ecosystem that we talked about earlier, our children should see that while we don't want family members to be dependent, we do want to be there for each other in true times of need.

You may be thinking, No, I don't want my kids to graduate with debt weighing on them. You are 100 percent correct, and it is terrible to do that to a kid. But find another way to avoid that situation that does not involve sinking yourself into debt. The only thing worse than a kid who can't get their life started because they have a ton of education-related debt is a parent who has to ask their adult kid for help because they blew their own nest egg to pay for college.

Make Sure They Are Doing the Math (Have a Budget)

One of my most memorable conversations with my college-age son was when he came to ask my husband and me for money to pay for his cost of living (in addition to college tuition). We asked him to let us know what he felt he needed and then to track his spending and let us know where the money was going. He was totally taken aback. He thought it was completely unfair that he had to tell us where exactly the money was going. I believe his specific words were, "I don't want to feel like a dependent."

But the truth is, he was a dependent and with that comes strings and expectations. For us, we have continued to expect to know where every penny is going if he wants us to reimburse him for basic expenses like food and household supplies while in school. He is responsible for what we would call "discretionary expenses" like going out with friends or entertainment.

But this is not a one-size-fits-all situation. Lieber recommends a generous but hands-off approach: "You come up with that monthly number, you multiply it times 12, and then you dump that amount in a lump sum into the bank account and say, talk to you in a year. No bailouts." Lieber explains that the child still has to get their basics but if he runs out of money, he will have to figure it out. And in Lieber's words, "That's just how it is going to go."

This is similar to what my own father did when I was a teenager. He would schedule a meeting with each of his three kids. We would sit in his study as he listened. Each of us would present him with our expected expenses for the semester, and we would discuss it. I had a habit of falling a bit short because when you are asking for money for a long stretch of time, it just seemed like too big a number to ask for. I always underestimated what my life cost. Generally, because I had part-time jobs in college, I was able to cover the gap. Remember, my generous dad was clear that the condition was that he was done after he wrote the check.

But the under-budgeting came to bite me when I went abroad my junior year of college. I did zero research on what it would cost to live in Paris, where I could not have a job to earn extra cash. Granted, this was before the internet so it's no longer as hard to research what it costs to live in different places. But I was so naive that I did not even think to research what it would cost to live in Paris, let alone travel to explore other places on the weekends. Looking back, of course I should have researched the additional costs and made my case to my father that I needed more money.

The end result was a lot of very inexpensive baguette and butter sandwiches, staying in zero-star youth hostels, and a very frugal semester abroad – which by the way was completely fine. I did not see asking my dad for more money as an option. I figured it out and managed and learned that in the future I needed to get more granular with my budgets and do the research with the tools that are available.

Don't Let Debt Be Their Dream Crusher

We now live in a world that is increasingly functioning on debt. For many young people, their first direct exposure is their own student debt. Many people sign on the dotted line before they or their parents fully understand what they are getting into. They are also offered credit cards and other loans regardless of any education on how those work. As we have discussed, many believe the minimum payments are what they are supposed to pay. Some young people tell me they believe the best way to build credit is to always carry some debt. This is of course completely false.

I still remember the story my friend David Bach shared from his college years. He has gone on to great success as an investment advisor and as author of the *Latte Factor* and 10 *New York Times* bestsellers. As a young adult, David built up debt in college, only to have his father pay it off. Rather than learn from the experience, he once again fell into debt. This time he was not bailed out. He had to earn the money to pay it off. Bach started a business and began to understand the impact of debt.

Paying Down Debt

At the end of the day, the best way to pay down debt if your young adult has it – credit card, student debt, or otherwise – is the one that works for your child. That said, some tried and true approaches are worth discussing with them.

I am personally a big fan of leveraging technology. I've worked with the team at Tally Technologies for a couple of years now because I believe their app simplifies and streamlines credit card debt repayment. In short, the Tally app will figure out the most efficient way to pay down debt and then set up automatic payments. If it makes sense financially and you qualify, they can also offer to consolidate debt into a lower cost line of credit.

Student loan debt can also be consolidated and refinanced by a number of companies. This can lower the interest rate and, depending on how the new loan is structured, lower the monthly payment. The big caveat is that if your child moves a federal loan into the private loan system, they may lose some key protections, so tread carefully.

There are also popular debt pay-down strategies that work for any kind of debt. Just like with diets, the best one is the one you will stick to. The snow-ball method focuses on paying off the smallest debt first. Extra money goes there while only the minimum goes to all the other debts. Once that is paid off, your child will move on to the next smallest and throw all the extra cash there. This is great for people who really need motivation. The avalanche method focuses on paying down the debt that is costing your child the most – meaning the one with the highest interest rate. It's the better financial deal because your child will pay less interest and probably be done more quickly. In general, though, many people find it harder to stick with this plan.

Talk with your child and make sure they have a plan that they can stick to and make sure to check in with them and give them some positive reinforcement. Any plan can and should be automated, and they can also make additional payments if they are able to make extra cash through side hustles, gifts from relatives, or through a raise or bonus at their job.

Major Decisions

Speaking of jobs, choosing a major can have a huge impact on your young adult's ability to pay off debt and earn a living in the years following graduation. I phrase it that way because for many of us, and especially for young people getting out of school today, there will be several careers. But this book is focusing on initial careers, so we'll start there.

Harrington stresses the important of knowing what a career's potential income is as part of the discussion when your child is choosing a major or a specialized educational program. Taking on huge debt for a career that won't support paying off a loan in a reasonable time frame should be a major red flag – pun intended. "I think that has a lot of bearing on how much debt students should take on and parents should take on," says Harrington. "If you've got a student who wants to major in computer science, for instance, they could probably both take the federal debt that's offered to them and possibly some private debt on top of it if they needed to, because their career outlook and their salary outlook is so much stronger than a teacher, for instance."

That reality hit home for my own daughter, who entered her university in the School of Education with plans to become a teacher and graduated four years later from the School of Informatics, Computing and Engineering. She wanted to have financial freedom, and while she really enjoyed working with kids as a camp counselor and lifeguard, the truth is she also wanted to have less stress about money. In her case she would not have had college debt regardless of her path. But after many talks with both her father and me, she simply concluded that she wanted a career with more financial upside than teaching. It would be nice if society valued teachers enough to make it more financially rewarding, but that was not an option for her at the time. If she had chosen a career in education, she would not have been able to save up enough money in two years not only to buy a home of her own but also to pay the mortgage and other ongoing associated expenses without being dependent on her parents.

This is grownup life, and it's our job as parents to help our kids make the best decisions for their priorities.

College Alternatives

While I am personally an advocate for college for most young people, there is a lot of discussion in our society about alternative educational paths. Capalad reminds us that the higher the cost of college climbs, the lower the relative financial return. "College costs are going up 5 percent every year. And if you compound that out 20 years, it's literally half a million dollars just to send a kid to undergrad. That's just not sustainable."

She says the math is a real eye-opener for her clients and suggests some serious thinking about what else could be done with the money that might have gone to pay for college. She suggests parents think carefully about always saving in a 529 plan, where parents have to use the money for educational expenses. For example, she says parents could encourage and help their kids to start a business or buy a house with those savings and have that financial security. "You have like companies like Google saying, 'We don't care if you have an undergrad degree; we just care that you can do the work.' I think a lot more companies are doing that. Can you actually do the work? Do you have the experience?"

Most of all, she says whether kids are going to college or not, they have to have jobs to learn firsthand the expectations and realities of the working world. That is a key part of education regardless of classroom education.

Review

1. Debt, deployed properly, can be a valuable tool in starting a financial grownup life.
2. Let your kids know that while you will not pay their debt, if they are in financial trouble they can and should come to you for advice and guidance. Be ready with specific ways they can pay down debt.
3. Be transparent about your own financial obligations, including debt.
4. Help your young adult project forward how they will pay down any debt they take on to finance their education, taking career choices into account.
5. Let them know that there are alternatives to college and the debt that comes with it.

CHAPTER 5

Career Foundations

I don't want other people to decide who I am. I want to decide that for myself.

— Emma Watson

Most of us parents want our kids to live their dreams – not ours – when it comes to their careers. But parents also have a responsibility to help their kids understand the connection between what they study, what it costs, and what they will earn as early as possible. This applies especially to graduate school, where many advanced degrees in liberal arts often lead to low-paying careers. The catch: If we as parents don't carefully listen to what they want to do and try to ram a career choice down their neck, they will tune us out. So there is a nuanced strategy to this. Passions often can pay more if we help our child pick the right career niche that is still tied to that passion.

Artist Andy Warhol famously worked as a commercial illustrator for about a decade before his career in art took off. It paid the bills and supported his life as an adult. It should also be noted that his exposure to the advertising world planted the seeds of his personal work depicting the material goods we use in our daily lives. Warhol is also a good example of how parents can be assets to helping their kids get their careers off the ground. Fun fact: Some of the shoe ads that Andy Warhol created in the late 1950s for I. Miller included captions by his mother, Julia Warhola.

Realistic lifestyle expectations are also important. A friend wanted to be a stay-at-home parent. Her husband wanted to have a predictable job that allowed him to remain in a band, play gigs at and occasionally travel. They chose to move to a more affordable area of the country. Those choices help to fund a lifestyle that allowed them to pursue what was most important to them, without being dependent on their parents.

Many parents want their kids to live near them and in a lifestyle in their twenties that is comparable to how the parents live in their forties, fifties, and sixties. We need to remind ourselves that odds are we have upgraded our lifestyle over the years. Most of us have felt a sense of accomplishment as this has happened, and we can do things like increasing our savings and investments or lift our lifestyle in whatever matters most to us as we go through our own adulting milestones. Parents often are the ones putting subtle pressure on their kids to be a step ahead of where they really are economically. We'll talk more about this later.

Focus on Your Own Listening Skills

Don't jump to conclusions and assume because your child wants to do something you don't know much about, it's not a good idea. Think about it: many jobs that are extremely lucrative and promising simply did not exist when you were planning your career strategy. In fact, many of us didn't even deliberately plan our careers, so we need to hold back a bit before we throw out a bunch of judgmental advice when we hear our kids want to be YouTubers or that the most important thing for them is a job that reflects their values and will promote a better world. They may not have dollar signs at the top of their list, but that doesn't mean they aren't aware of the need for income. They just may not have that as their top priority. And don't forget: priorities may change as your child goes through life.

This is a common struggle in families in which the children are first-generation Americans. Parents are focused on security and have often taken big risks for their children to have a chance at a better life. In these families, the parents want their kids to work in professions that are safe and, in their mind, guaranteed to provide financial security and community acceptance. That's why you hear so much about parents in previous generations wanting their kids to be doctors and lawyers. The perception is that if their kid follows that career path, there is no risk. Unfortunately, that is no longer true. For example, if a child genuinely wants to be a doctor, that can be an incredible career and well worth pursuing. But getting there will likely be extremely expensive no matter how it is funded. There are not just years of school and training involved but also many years of lost income, potential debt accumulation, and of course lifestyle choices. At the same time, the medical business – and it is a business – is in a period of transition. There is strong demand for medical professionals, but it is not limited to doctors. Costs like insurance and overhead can be very high for doctors, and for many their income upside is not as much as they had expected.

So, sticking with medicine, rather than insist your child become a doctor, listen to their interests and ask about their plans and concerns. Who would pay for all the years of school and relatively low income? How well does the area of medicine that they want to go into pay? How ready are they to put the work in to get there including giving up a lot of the "fun" of being a young adult? What are the risks of not getting into various specialty programs they may be interested in following? How do they hope to be compensated: will they have to want up their own private practice, or will they work as an employee? How many years would they carry the debt, and how would that impact their ability to afford the life they may want – potentially including a partner and a family? You could open the discussion to other areas of health care that could be lucrative in a way that interests your child just as much or more and can also fit their income and lifestyle goals. They might look into being an executive at a health care company, or if they want to be patient facing, a career as a nurse practitioner could be an idea. Websites like Indeed.com and Monster.com can be great resources to research average pay for different careers.

Licensed mental health counselor Janine Halloran specializes in working with children and teens on social and coping skills and is the author of several books, including *Coping Skills for Teens*. She cautions parents to also separate their bias and perceptions when their kids come to them with their career aspirations. For example, Halloran has a neighbor who wasn't thrilled that her daughter wanted to be a hairdresser. She worried it would limit her opportunities and her income. Halloran says this is an example of how we as parents tie our judgments about jobs to our own identity – at the risk of alienating our kids. We also might be flat-out wrong. "She makes bank as a hairdresser – like so much money. But it's not a career that people necessarily think of as something that is lucrative."

If your kids want a job that is not going to support the lifestyle you believe they are planning on, it is important to have that discussion up front. There is plenty of information readily available about what various careers will pay, and the cost of living in different areas of the country. Give them the facts, and then let them sink in. Not all decisions need to be made right away, and what they want to do now can change quite a bit as they continue to grow into adulthood. No one job or career path needs to be forever. Halloran says, "It's hard for us to sit back and be like, okay, I think that I can see the future and I can see how this is going to play out. But truthfully, the days of like getting a degree and getting a job and staying at a job for 30 years are over; it doesn't happen anymore."

Let's circle back to the ever popular career choice of YouTuber. I personally know a 14-year-old who lives in my home right now who is incredibly interested in this so-called career. Can you see my eyes rolling? On the other hand, who am I to say he's not going to make it? My strategy so far is to ask questions, listen, and wait and see. When I ask about what is driving his interest, my son explains that he feels the YouTubers he watches have a really big impact on the world. For example, he says that Mr. Beast raised tens of millions to save and plant trees. What this tells me is I have a kid who wants to do good. I asked him how Mr. Beast actually makes money, and he explained that he gets donations to sponsor his content. He also streams ads on his content, which generates income, he explained. In other words, while I have plenty of reservations about my child becoming a YouTuber, it would be wrong to assume he has not thought of the importance of generating income from his career choice.

I would also be wrong to assume his obsession with video games is not something that could lead to a career choice. For example, in the past we might have thought that a high school kid who aced the SATs could become an SAT tutor and earn money working part-time while in school. The truth is that these days young people can also make money teaching younger kids video game skills at after-school classes and in camps. They can also work as consultants to gaming companies looking for feedback and game development support. Coding skills are always in demand and can lead to bigger opportunities in the industry.

My point is, before we push them into the career fields we think are "safer" or more "realistic," we should all take the time to hear them out. If there is true talent and work ethic, we should help them create a path to profit from their passion, talk them through where the money is in the industry of their choice, and help them identify ways to do more than just enjoy being a consumer and move toward being an owner.

Liz Weston adds that what people can get paid to do as a career is constantly changing; we just have to help make sure our kids are ready. "We should just keep that mind that we cannot predict what jobs are going to be there, what skills are going to be important."

Negotiation Skills Are Nonnegotiable

Teaching our young adults to negotiate is essential especially when they are getting their first job. That first salary can serve as a benchmark for future raises both at that company and beyond. But it can also be the toughest one to negotiate for a few reasons.

I remember trying to negotiate my first real full-time job offer. It was at CNBC, and when I asked if they could do better on the offer, I was shut down immediately. My future boss said simply, "You are right out of college. You have zero experience in a full-time job. You are lucky to be even offered a full-time job with benefits. We'll see you on Monday." Then she hung up the phone. And yes, I showed up on Monday.

Pam Capalad is not surprised. "You might get shot down on your first job. You probably will. But having the experience of asking for more and advocating for yourself, especially in a first job, no one told me that I could, I didn't even know I could negotiate. I feel like that was, that was such a big learning curve for me, that I was even allowed to ask." But that doesn't mean it's not worth helping our kids learn to advocate for themselves and try.

For example, when I was starting my business, my friend's daughter was looking for a paid internship. I had known her for years and thought she would be a great fit. Before I interviewed her, I spoke to my friend (her mom), and we decided to use the interview process to also help her daughter learn to negotiate. I told my friend that I was going to lowball her daughter and to make sure her daughter knew to counter and negotiate a better offer. As our interview wrapped up, I made her the offer for the internship. I kept a straight face, but inside I was of course hoping that she did not just accept and that she took her mom's advice and asked for more. And she did. I told her I had to think about it, and then the next day I came back with something in the middle.

Was it a somewhat artificial situation? Sure. But it was a way to have her daughter practice standing up for herself, negotiating, and then compromising. Think of ways you can help your child. It sounds forced. but acting out real-world scenarios can be effective, even if they are hesitant. Enlisting a friend who is in their field may also be a way to give them practice they can put to work when they need to.

Life Is Tough Enough – Make the Introductions (If You Can)

The truth is that life is not fair and nothing we as parents do is going to even the playing field. For most of us, we fall somewhere in the middle. We can't instantly create success for our kids, but we can do things along the way to increase their odds of success.

It's tempting to complain that so-and-so's child had this advantage or that we wish we had had a family business to go into – the list goes on. Your kids may come to you and let you know that one of their classmates or friends is getting a fantastic internship at the most glamorous and exciting place ever created on earth. While that is probably an exaggeration, the truth is some young adults absolutely do get a head start. The vast majority of young adults also do not get that head start and do not have everything handed to them. Many struggle to figure out how to even break into the industry of their choice.

Side note: make no mistake. Those head starts can also backfire. People know when someone got a position because they were the boss's child or whatever. Odds are they will be under intense scrutiny. If the person can't do the job, it will become clear very quickly and can sometimes backfire.

The world is not fair. It probably wasn't fair when you were a young adult, and it still is stacked against many people. Racism, sexism, and other biases still exist even though progress is being made. That's why I advocate for using any advantage you may have that you can offer your child to help them get to a place where they can succeed. Be realistic about their skills and what they can offer. If your child loves singing but is tone-deaf, don't burn bridges trying to get them an audition through a friend of a friend of a friend. Where there is talent and drive, though, get creative with how you can help them stand out and connect with potential opportunities.

Here's an example. If you know of someone who works in an industry that your child would like to break into, reach out and ask if your child can come in and shadow them for a day. Don't limit it to your immediate circle or to people who are high up in the company. Do a lot of asking. You may have friends with children in that industry who you don't even realize could be a key connection. The ask doesn't cost the friend anything and may even flatter them. They can meet your child without pressure. The age to start this will vary depending on your child's maturity, how well developed their interest is, and your own personal comfort level.

The most important thing in that situation is to make sure your child is prepared and has the right mindset for the experience. Don't send them without making sure they understand what to expect and how to behave in this possibly new and uncomfortable situation. That can be as basic as making sure they are on time; have studied up on the person, the company, and the industry so they can engage in conversations; and are excited about the opportunity. This is their chance to make a preemployment impression, and first impressions count. Your friend will be assessing them and will likely be thinking about how they can help them break into the industry. It's human nature to want to help. So your child needs to be somewhat aware of the stakes without putting so much pressure on them that they freak out.

The advantage (and disadvantage in some cases) of this approach is that it can feel like less pressure. It's not even an informational interview. It's just a chance to see how a business in their industry of choice works and what a typical day is like at an office. So much of success at work is tied to our ability to adapt to the expectations and culture of the company community, and spending time in an office can be very helpful to get a clear perspective on all of that. The fact that in the postpandemic world we will all likely work independently some of the time makes this informal mentorship exposure even more important. We need to make sure our kids know that even if a boss is not there hovering over them and checking in as they walk by during the day, they are still "at work" when they work at home.

Make sure they know how to dress for the day. Don't assume they know what they are doing. Many young people will push to wear what they feel is the best expression of themselves. If that is also appropriate, you're good.

But be firm if you must interfere. This is also a reflection of you. Generally, the best outfit is a balance between what the employees wear and what they feel comfortable in. I have had young people spend the day with me in the newsroom at the request of friends and they come in dressed inappropriately – it is not good.

I remember when I expressed an interest in public speaking, my dad arranged for me to help the head of public relations at his firm at an event the company was holding for investors. I spent the day assisting her with a variety of tasks and errands ranging from checking people in when they arrived, to passing microphones around during the conference. It was just one day, but the impact was huge. I have kept in touch with her loosely over the years as she left that firm and built her own powerhouse agency. In 2014 when I had an idea for a book and wanted someone to give me feedback, she not only took my call but also welcomed me to meet with her in person several times over the course of my brand development for Financial Grownup. Her advice and support were priceless. It meant the world to me to see her at my book launch party in 2016, decades after we met.

Be sure to offer to return the favor to friends and ask if they would like for you to host their kids one day if your profession is of interest. If that is not a match, a nice token thank-you gift is appropriate, as is a follow-up thank-you note from your child. Encourage your child to send updates to the potential mentor at regular intervals to build a relationship before there is an ask. I have personally been terrible at this and regret many potential relationships that were lost simply through the passage of time and the lack of consistent follow-up. It's hard. But that's why keeping in touch can be such a huge advantage. So few people do it!

I often take meetings with young people who want to get into journalism, and while they thank me at the time and often send a thank-you note, I generally never hear from them again. I would be more than willing to help them, but they don't ask. So please encourage your kids to put a recurring reminder in their digital calendar, maybe once a quarter to keep up with these older adults who can be mentors.

Leveraging Skills

We learned during the pandemic to be resourceful and to think about different ways to leverage the skills we were using from our jobs in the before. Young people have dreams that we want to nurture. But they also have bills that we need to make sure they to learn to pay without our help. Sometimes that means finding income that is adjacent to their dream jobs and careers.

A perfect example is my 21-year-old. He is studying TV and film in college and dreams of being a movie director. He is determined and talented. But most likely he will not have income from directing a major feature film when he graduates from college in a year. This summer, as I write this book, he is working at a public relations firm. Why? Well, because he is helping them create content. Content creation is a hot field right now as social media expands, marketing and advertising go through huge shifts, and of course the streaming networks are pumping out more content than ever. On the surface, creating content to help grow a company is very different from a feature film. But content is content.

My son is also learning that while the quality of the content is essential, it is a product that still will need to be marketed to have financial success. Most likely when he graduates he will have to have a job that has consistent income at a company. The interpersonal skills he is learning will be crucial. The connections he is making and the recommendations I hope for him to have will be door openers. And while it may be tough, his personal film projects will likely be his side hustle until he is able to find a way to monetize his passion and transform it into a profit.

The pandemic also took away excuses tied to logistics like transportation and created new opportunities to earn income as a side hustle while still pursuing a passion. An aspiring musician can teach music online and earn a pretty penny; trust me, I paid quite a bit to my younger son's drum teacher over the past year and a half! Opportunities are everywhere for extra income, and the satisfaction kids get from that success will drive them to even more creative ways to leverage their talents.

Do the Math and Do the Budgets

What if your kid says they don't care about money and are not materialistic? Listen to their reasons first. Then try to ask questions that will hopefully uncover something they do want that costs money. For example, they may say they really want to have a dog. Those cost money – not just adopting one but also the ongoing costs. They may want to travel. Go through their wants. Then bring up their needs. These are things that you may be paying for right now. They may think they don't need health care, but you should explain why they do need it. At the very least, they probably do want to eat food. This is the time to break out the calculator and start showing them what their so-called minimalist life actually costs.

There are several different ways to create a budget and figure out what their grownup life will cost. I prefer to keep it simple. Have them write down everything they spend for three months. You should also write down all your expenses tied to them for the same period. Then compare notes and do the math so they can see what their life actually costs. As they get older, consider using a budgeting app to help them track their spending. Make sure they understand the costs that you cover when they are part of your household that will be their responsibility as financial grownups.

Living Their Best Life – Not Yours

By the time our kids are starting their careers, odds are we have a lifestyle that is much better economically than it was when we were at that life stage. We often forget the back-of-the-building, first-floor studio apartments or the up-and-coming neighborhood crash pad we shared with a gaggle of room-mates with whom we ate ramen noodles in our early twenties. We want our kids to be comfortable. We don't want them to downgrade their lifestyle especially as we see them working so hard in their career.

There is nothing wrong with financial generosity. There is also nothing wrong with some support as long as you have an exit strategy and are not expected to offer your support indefinitely.

CERTIFIED FINANCIAL PLANNER™ practitioner Cynthia Meyer of Real Life Planning warns us that we need to make sure we don't artificially boost their ongoing basic lifestyle to one they can't possibly maintain on their own. It can lead to them feeling inadequate and not living up to your expectations of success. She says it's crucial that parents of young adults are "making sure that they know that their lifestyle has to be based on their income, not your income. What I see a lot, especially with affluent families is, you know, kids get into college and then they get their first job, and they think they should live like Mommy and Daddy."

In many cases, living like Mom and Dad is not going to be realistic, and we should avoid putting young adults in situations where they feel they have to keep up. For example, if they ask for a restaurant recommendation and you are at a point in your life where you can go to pricey places, that does not mean you should suggest that they splurge – even if you think they deserve it. Don't suggest retail therapy when your child is feeling down. Don't push them to go on an expensive vacation. Don't suggest they adopt a dog that will push their budget to the limit.

This may seem obvious as you read it, but as parents start to relate to their kids in less formal ways, it does happen without us being aware of the expectations we put on young adults to live a lifestyle that is not realistic.

Review

1. Encourage your kids to follow their passion in a way that it will put them on a path to pay for the lifestyle they want.
2. Don't unintentionally push your kids to keep up with your lifestyle. Meet them at their level so they can have the satisfaction of financial separation.
3. Focus on your listening skills when it comes to their career choices, and be open-minded about new ways to earn a living.
4. Make sure they know they can and should negotiate.
5. Life is tough enough: make introductions and offer career help if asked.
6. Help self-proclaimed nonmaterialistic kids understand that not wanting stuff has little to do with financial self-sufficiency so they will have economic choices.

CHAPTER 6

Homeroom

This was not the landing pad; this was the launching pad.
—Tonya Rapley, financial educator and Founder,
My Fab Finance, on moving home as a young adult

The whole idea of the young adult generation moving out is a relatively new one – and still not common in many cultures. For much of history, many generations lived together in one residence, with good reason. Not only are there economic efficiencies of sharing the space, but families also often enjoy being with each other and offer support through the challenges life inevitably brings. The reality is that for most parents – who want to live financially independent lives themselves as they get older and retire – one goal is to get their adult children out of their childhood home and into a home of their own.

Pushing them out too fast and without the right financial education and a sustainable foundation can backfire, though. We as parents need to tread carefully even if having an adult, who happens to be your child, as a house-mate is not our ideal.

Let the Boomerang Begin

Graduation from school – high school, college, or graduate school – is a big milestone for our kids. It also means figuring out where they are going to live after the big day, and this depends on whether they have a source of income lined up by the time they graduate. If they don't, then in most cases the decision is simple: they are moving home unless you are going to pay for them to not live at home. Completely funding your child's life without any contribution from them can be both financially precarious for you and impede your child's path to becoming a financial grownup – unless there is some really good reason they can't land a job.

If your child does have a source of income, it could give them a solid financial foundation if they move home and save up money with specific milestones and goals. Even with income, if they go right from college into some kind of housing where they are paying monthly bills, they likely won't have things like an emergency fund and a strong credit rating that will serve them well if they make a relatively brief stop in their childhood homes. There are infinite variables and considerations, so this is ultimately going to be a personal choice tied in large part to the child's personality and everyone's resources, needs, and goals.

For the purposes of discussion, let's focus on the scenario of them moving home for a period of time with the expectation that it will have a defined purpose and duration. In this case, it is essential that parents set up rules and expectations for how things will work. Assuming everyone is on the same page without talking about it first could easily cause things to spiral quickly. As everyone settles into the new normal, there may be unexpected speed bumps. The last time your offspring lived at home, they were probably underage minor children. Everyone runs their home differently, but for many families their kids' contributions were limited to chores and cleaning up after themselves. They may have received allowance. They may have had a job, but they probably did not pay you rent. The same goes for chipping in for the groceries and other everyday household expenses. In fact, they were probably barely aware of how much it was costing you, their parents, to run a household.

Many of us Gen X parents clean up to some extent after our kids, make most of the meals, do their laundry, and ask very little of them except for them to study and get good grades, attend activities we often pay for, maybe do some volunteer work, and of course have fun with their friends. We rationalize that we just want them to be happy. We want them to have the most perfect childhoods possible because we know adult life can be tough. Why not protect them as long as possible? It's also usually easier for us and avoids conflict that we don't want to add to our own overscheduled lives. And let's not forget, we want them to like us. Many of us secretly want our kids to approve of the job we are doing as their parents. I'm so guilty of this. When my teenage son makes a mess, I know it's best for him to clean it up himself. That is always the goal. But I'd be lying if I said there weren't times when I was exasperated and just picked up the damn pajamas off the floor and put them in the laundry basket because I just didn't want to ask him yet again. We are so tired as parents. This is not good – and it undermines our goal to get them to clean up after themselves – literally and figuratively. But in the moment, it's so hard.

Oh, and did I mention we are tired?

To some degree, we as parents are looking to our kids and even to our communities for validation that we did a good job – and we are still needed. That it's not over. It's like we want a trophy for parenting – just like we want the likes on social media. We want to matter. We want to retain our place of importance and not give up our starring role in our kids' lives for fear of becoming bit players or – gasp – being relegated to cameos.

I have been guilty of reaching out to teachers and asking, on behalf of my child, without him asking, for extra credit work he could do to bring up a grade! I could not bear his getting a grade that did not reflect his exceptional intelligence just because he didn't hand in the assignment on time.

We invest so much in our children; we often take their success as our success – and the reverse when they come up short. Ultimately, though, this
undermines our children. We need to own up to the fact that we are often
the ones at fault. To learn from failures, a child has to first be allowed to fail.

Rules + Expectations = Launch

Our homes should not be democracies. We need to remain in charge as
parents, even as our relationship evolves when our kids get older. They are
not our roommates or our friends. They are still our children. We are still
responsible to launch them into adulthood. Our interactions will be different, but they are living in *our* home. It's still our rules even though they have
celebrated a few more birthdays since they last lived here.

Attorney Leslie Tayne believes in setting boundaries. "I do not let my
children . . . rule my roost. I have many people say I'm very strict. I just
see myself as parenting. I definitely make the separation between parent
and child." When Tayne's kids moved home during the pandemic, she was
very clear on her expectations. She did not suddenly start ordering in dinner
when the kids were asking for it – even though she could have afforded it.
But she also realized a crucial upside to having adult children at home. The
unexpected family time opened up opportunities for some frank discussions
about money and future financial obligations. "My older daughter who is finishing school asked me to pull up the federal student loan so she could look
at it and start thinking about how she is going to budget to pay for it." She
and her husband held their ground with their children when they asked for
financial support during the pandemic. "If you want to stay home, it's totally
fine. But you have to pay for the apartment. If you're working remotely, if
you want that apartment, then you have to go back to school. And every one
of our kids went back to school and stayed at school."

Financial educator Tonya Rapley, founder of My Fab Finance, advises parents
of kids who have moved home to take the initiative in helping their kids
move out – and stresses that it does not have to involve direct financial help.
"There are ways you can support someone without giving money financially:
'Hey, do you want to go look at some apartments? You want to start looking
at a house? Do you have any questions about buying a house? Do you want
to have a look at your credit score, your down payment? Do you have a bank
account to put this in?'" She says having those conversations lets your kids
know that you're invested in their successful exit from the family home and
that you are a source of knowledge and support for them.

Our memories tend to be short, but the need for a little nudge out the door is not unique to our children. Remember, Gen X was known as the slacker generation. But think about that. Young adults who lived at home were considered slackers. Now the stigma is all but gone. We need to ask ourselves: Is removing the societal and peer pressure to create a home of their own a completely good thing?

Our kids deserve a grownup life, too, and the truth is that they often need our help to get to the point where, frankly, they don't need our help. As Rapley points out, that help does not always mean financial support; it can also come in the form of guidance and some tough love about choices and coming to accept a realistic lifestyle for where they are in their life and their career.

As a young adult, Rapley was on the other side of the table; she moved home for financial reasons and would have liked her parents to have held her accountable for her financial decisions while she was living with them. "My parents weren't really involved in my financial decision-making, even though I was living in their house." Rapley regrets not putting more money into savings and building up her credit score. She also remembers cashing out a 401(k) with about $1,100 in it and not having a conversation with her parents first about what do with it. She wishes she had known about the option to roll it over into an IRA or that when it finally landed in her bank account it would be only about $800 instead of the full amount. She now understands that her parents, who were both military veterans, had two retirement incomes available to them and so had done little financial planning for those years.

Even if you yourself don't have to be hands-on with your money, you do need to have the conversations with your kids so they know that you care, that you are vested in their future financial success, and that you believe in them. In many ways, it all goes back to the family financial ecosystem we discussed earlier.

Rapley also reminds us that there are everyday life skills we can teach our children just by keeping them close. If an adult child is living at home, this could be a great way to both teach them and bond. She points out that this can be as simple as bringing them to the bank or the grocery story. Open the mail with them there, show them investment statements, and walk them through your investment accounts. You can show them how your retirement accounts have grown or how much the government takes out of your paycheck.

If you're hesitant to show your kids your finances, it is okay to be selective. But if we don't push the issue, the damage could snowball as the years go by, when we can no longer provide the support they have come to be dependent on for so many years. We also risk depleting our own financial resources and potentially needing to rely on them for support.

Tayne says she sees parents supporting adult children well into their twenties and thirties. One client came to her for help because her house was going into foreclosure. Tayne suggested she sell it since she didn't need a large home now that her children were grown. Then the truth came out: her adult kids were still living there! While they occasionally contributed financially, there was no specific, documented, and regular financial payment that she could count on.

Lieber is adamant we lay down the rules and expectations from the start. "Right before your kids move back home, you know, to save money, you need to get super granular about what your expectations are," he says. "Especially if they're living rent-free." He adds that we need to be very specific and not take anything for granted or assume they understand that living at home as an adult will be under very different terms. "What does that mean? What their responsibilities are, or do they have to you, what privileges do you have to peer into their lives or their livelihood? There should be some negotiation and conversation around that and not just implicit understanding you're living here rent-free."

For example, you might want to let them know that you will be looking at their bank account and their spending if you are providing any financial support, including free housing. If they push back, hold your ground. You may change your terms as their stay at home continues. If you pay their phone bill, you must have access to see what is going on there. In other words, if you pay the bill, you see the bill. End of story.

Julie Lythcott-Haims, author of *Your Turn: How to Be an Adult*, stresses that parents need to have the confidence in their own parenting competence to believe their kids will be okay if they are not in the picture. She emphasizes that we need to step back and give them the space to see what it costs to be them. "Your child is not appreciating the actual expenses associated with maintaining a life. You are making it seem easier than it is. And that's problematic." Lythcott-Haims says parents who consistently prevent their kids from understanding their own personal economics are buying themselves a permanent role – and that is ultimately going to hurt their kids. "If you don't transfer it over to them, you're propping them up," she warns. "You better have all the funds necessary to prop them up forever with a bequest after you die, because you're failing to teach them to do for themselves."

Licensed mental health counselor Janine Halloran has seen parents fail to give their kids the space to fail. "We actually need to let them have those moments of failure. We need to have them struggle. And it is extremely challenging to watch, to sit at the sidelines and know if I step in, I can make it better." Halloran clarifies that if something is going to have a huge, gigantic impact on their lives, we as parents should use our best judgment and step in but that little financial mistakes have to happen so they can figure out how to solve them on their own. We also have to be patient and give them the space to learn from life. "It's hard because we want to have the conversation and we want to fix it and finish it all in one fell swoop," says Halloran. "And that is not how life works. We have to do it in chunks so that it's over time."

Lythcott-Haims adds that parents are giving them a crutch that they are hanging on to so they can't learn to walk on their own. At the same time, she worries parents are undermining their own financial situation. This can also do psychological damage when children don't have confidence in their own ability to function as adults. "When somebody lacks autonomy in their life, they're basically managed, handled by someone else. Research is increasingly showing this leads to anxiety. This leads to depression."

How parents communicate this is essential. It should be done firmly but also in a way that lets them know you are confident in their ability to live in your home not as a child but as an adult member of the family and that these expectations are there specifically because even though you love them as a parent, you believe in their ability to be an adult member of the family and to embrace that role.

There Has to Be a Timeline

This is going to vary with every child and will be dependent on the reason not only for their moving home but also their moving out. It is absolutely necessary to have a conversation right when they move in – and possibly before then – about the expected time period they will live at home, their plan to make the best use of this season of their life, and the goal they need to reach to move out.

Grown and Flown's Mary Dell Harrington reminds us that the consequences of not setting them up for launching early on can lead to some very tough times. "If they're a young adult that continues to come back to you, time after time, and has not yet gotten their income in line with their expenses, there has to be a moment when that just can't continue. That's undoubtedly a very painful moment for everybody involved."

Review

1. Set up rules and expectations immediately when an adult child moves home. Do not make assumptions that there is an understanding.
2. Be cognizant that your child is an adult, and their contributions to the household should be adjusted to reflect that.
3. Give your kids the space to fail.
4. Regardless of age, you are still their parent and not their peer.
5. Have a timeline, and if it is adjusted, make sure there is clear communication and specific expectations for an exit strategy.

CHAPTER 7

(Lifestyle) Inflation

Money looks better in the bank than on your feet.
—Sophia Amoruso, Founder, Girlboss Media

The urge to splurge as they get older grows exponentially for our kids as they grow up. We may think we can relate, but the truth is there are new and powerful forces at play that are influencing our kids' spending – including influencers. Think of it as peer pressure on steroids that calls to them 24 hours a day.

Our young adults are online and on social media all the time. They are digital natives and have zero life experience before smartphones. According to Pew Research, 84 percent of young adults ages 18–29 years are online.[1] Money flows freely on apps like Venmo and Zelle. In fact, many teens are on social media, where on most platforms the age requirement is 13, before they even have their own bank account at age 18. (Note: They should have a teen bank account, which we as parents set up with them and can monitor.)

According to Influencer Marketing Hub, over 70 percent of teens say they think YouTubers are more reliable than celebrities.[2] They see them as more relatable and real. We can't be in denial: there are powerful forces at play that will drive both our child's and their peers' spending decisions. The content they see on social media is powerful and has the potential to drive lifestyle inflation well before they have the means to keep up. Let's also take note that while our shopping options growing up were limited to physical stores that would actually be closed at times, our kids are exposed to shopping opportunities 24/7 though their phones and other devices. There is never a time when they can't hit the Buy button and get that retail fix.

Odds are they are being pitched not by a child actor in a television commercial talking about cereal like we were but by a YouTube star sharing with them why they *love* a certain product and they really want all their friends to have it – because they care. Make no mistake, that link your kid clicks to take them to the online checkout ensures the influencer gets a cut of what the customer spends. Add in the normal pressures of teenage life, and our kids are prime targets. Not surprisingly, young adults are on social media even more since the coronavirus pandemic started, according to a recent survey conducted by Barnes & Noble College Insights of 1,108 college students ages 18–24 years.[3] And while more browse than buy, the 2020 study found that almost half (47 percent) of Gen Z college students who follow brands on Instagram have made a purchase through that platform, and 72 percent were more likely to buy from a brand they follow on social. The temptation for that quick retail fix is real and shows no signs of slowing down.

Early Adulting with Money

Family finance expert Andy Hill, who hosts the *Marriage Kids & Money* podcast, worries that as kids move out of college dorms or our homes and start earning grownup money, the excitement over the spending power they get could get out of control fast. "They just left college where they were eating ramen noodles and pizza, and all of a sudden they're making 60, 70, 80, whatever out of college. And man, they could get that car. They can buy that house. They can go to the club; they can go on vacations with their friends." And they *can* do all those things. But odds are they may not yet fully appreciate all the adult things they *must* do: like pay all their bills, build an emergency fund, and start saving up for not just retirement but also short- and medium-term goals.

I want to take a moment to note that I chose to include this topic as part of the core curriculum, before our teens and young adults get that first big grownup paycheck (which we'll go over soon) and experience the potential pitfalls that come along with it. We as parents need to manage expectations about their lifestyle at this stage of their life, keeping in mind the heavy influence of social media.

Hill wishes he had gotten the memo on that. "I remember my unrealistic expectation when I graduated college. I was just like, Hey, whatever my parents have, I want that immediately," he says. "They have a luxury car, so I'm going to lease one at 22 years old because why not? I need an Audi."

It's not just about the spending everything they are earning (and sometimes more), potentially leading to debt issues and other troubles to the downside; it is also about missing the upside including amplified investment opportunities because of the sheer number of years they have ahead of them for their money to grow. Add to that the "free money" they can get from their employers each year – if they take the time to understand what is available, and follow up by making sure they are contributing what is required to get the most value from those programs.

Hill still looks back on his own personal choices with regret. "Some of those things that I wish that I would have done when I was 21 or 22, right out of college, is take advantage of free money from my employer through a 401(k) match, or actually some employers now are given an HSA match, which is fantastic, a great way to save."

Cynthia Meyer, CERTIFIED FINANCIAL PLANNER™ professional with Real Life Planning, points out that for parents it is also a question of doing the math, seeing that it won't add up, and taking a firm stand. "I mean, unless you're planning to subsidize their lifestyle, they will be taking a lifestyle step down. Right. Because what somebody makes in their twenties is not going to be what somebody makes in their fifties"

Adulting Milestones Are Expensive

One of the toughest financial pressures for a lot of young adults these days is actually tied to the adulting milestone of getting married. While the pandemic did give many of us the time and space to step back and put the often over-the-top wedding celebration in perspective, the truth is they are already coming back, along with the sky-high price tags not just for the couple but for everyone involved.

Even being a bridesmaid or groomsman in a wedding can have steep costs. *HerMoney*'s Jean Chatzky has observed these effects with the young women on her team who are in their friends' weddings. Her daughter has told her that the gift-giving has also become more expensive – with even the bride and groom buying very expensive gifts for their wedding party. "I'm thinking, you know, where is this money all coming from? This is insane. And maybe it's in part that the people in the wedding party are having to spend so much money. I think in part you've got to set expectations with your friends."

Chatzky advises parents to talk to their kids about setting boundaries with their friends. "When you say yes to these things, say, 'I will happily be in your wedding. I can totally afford to fly out for the shower, but I'm not going to be able to do the shower and the bachelorette.'"

When and How to Step In

Once our young adults are spending their own money, not ours, there are limits to what we can do to protect them from bad spending decisions. We also have to accept that they also may have different priorities. What we see as a mistake may be them living their best lives for where they want to be right now. It's important for parents to reserve judgment and give their kids the space to make their own decisions.

Tori Dunlap of My First 100k warns parents: "We're not going to listen to it, or we're going to shut down immediately and we're just going to go, okay, you don't know anything about us or our lives." She says to avoid telling kids they are doing something wrong or that it doesn't align with the parents' values, and to avoid being accusatory or having a confrontation. Instead, she advises them to have a conversation and take an approach like this:

"I noticed you're spending a lot of money on bars or whatever (insert situation here). But I also know travel's really important to you. And, you know, something that I've realized in my own life is that I really enjoy spending money on things that I love. But if I spend my money here, that means I can't spend it on something else."

Dunlap says to just present it casually as food for thought – and not to force the issue even if you don't share your child's priorities. She also reminds parents that their actions will speak louder than their words. "I've seen with so many of my clients that their parents would tell them don't overspend on credit cards, and then they would watch them. They would watch their parents actively overspend on credit cards."

Review

1. Social media ups the ante when it comes to spending temptations.
2. There are new peer pressure–driven spending expectations tied to adulting milestones like weddings.
3. Young adults want to feel successful and use money to express their new status as adults.
4. Many of our kids aspire to lifestyles that are not realistic for where they are in their career and in their life.
5. Be thoughtful and use a supportive tone when approaching your young adult about their money choices.

Graduate Studies

CHAPTER 8

Exit Strategy: Getting Your Kids to Pay Their Own Bills

We are in the grownup-making business.
—Ron Lieber, "Your Money" *New York Times* columnist and author of *The Price You Pay for College*

On the surface, the concept seems simple: Once your children have income, they should pay their bills as much as possible. As an academic exercise we can rattle off all the bills they should pay when they get their first job: their phone, their car (if they have one) or other means of transportation, their spending money for going out with friends, and so on.

But for a generation of helicopter parents, it can be complicated. If you need to push them off "the payroll" for your own financial reasons, you have to decide if and how you want to let them know that it's not actually a choice for you. Many parents want to remain a source of security and strength for kids. It's natural for us parents to not want our children at any age to think we are vulnerable in any area of our life – including financially vulnerable. And if parents do have the money to comfortably pay those bills, the situation has other complications. The parent isn't saying they can't pay the bills; they are saying they *won't*. That can cause resentment if it is not presented and received well.

This is where mindset can be helpful. We as parents can often benefit by reframing our thinking on what is a gift to kids and what is not. On the surface, we might think gifts are things we buy for them. But the gift of confidence in their ability to fend for themselves should not be overlooked.

Allison Task, parenting coach and author of *Personal (R)evolution,* who earlier in the book shared the experience of her client who wanted her daughter to earn and pay for – as she called it – "her first shitty car," reminds us that parents often "derive our power and sense of contribution from making people's lives easier, but you're just not giving them skills they really need."

Take a moment to picture the smile on your child's face if you presented them with a brand-new car that you picked out for them. No matter how much they appreciate it and how nice it is, it would always be something you gave them. And off they go! How would they take care of it and maintain it? How *invested* in it would they be?

Now picture them working and saving up to buy a car themselves and then asking you to go along with them as they picked out the car and paid for it themselves. Watch them sit with pride as they tell the dealer, yes, they are the buyer – not you. You listen and help them ask questions and do research. Would they pay closer attention to the terms of the loan or lease knowing they are on the hook? Would they be more selective with the options they choose? Would they ultimately end up in a vehicle that reflected their actual economic status – not yours?

Getting to that second scenario is much harder than just getting them a car, even if it's our old car we gift them. But we also know they will get so much more joy if they are in the driver's seat – metaphorically and literally. Isn't that the ultimate bragging rights for your kid? And since we live in the real world, there is a happy medium. It does not have to be all-or-nothing. If you do have the means, it might incentivize your child by saying if you match what they earn and contribute that toward their goal. But I promise you, making sure they have skin in the game will be a gift to your child.

Remember, a successful exit strategy has to involve us stepping back and letting them feel the pinch of the paycheck. In many cases, they will not get a clear picture of how limited their financial power is until they start earning money. Our children need to not just be told how far their money will go; they need to feel it and experience it for it to really sink in. That can be so hard to watch and equally hard to resist stepping in to cushion the blow.

Emotions and empathy for kids can play a big role. When my stepdaughter was 22, she got her first full-time job and earned her first big paycheck. It was exciting – until she opened it. Then came a deafening, ear-splitting primal scream. She had discovered that a massive percentage had been taken out for taxes, and despite having run the numbers in advance knowing this, there was far less left in the paycheck than she had anticipated. The numbers made it real and personal. Suddenly she understood how much of a premium it costs to live in New York City, where we pay federal, state, and city income taxes. She also quickly became familiar with the payroll tax. As her first year of employment continued, she learned about deductions for 401(k)s, her health care plan premiums, and contributions to her new health savings account.

Many of us parents are tempted to say a sarcastic "Told you so" for all the times our children may have overheard us complain about paying more and more for health care plans that seem to cover less and less and all the other things taken out of our paychecks before our actual take-home pay. Part of us wants to just give them a hug. Sometimes we want to write a check to make the stress go away. It is tempting to try to "make them whole" and give them the cash to make up for all that was taken out so unjustly. If you are reading this and think that is farfetched, you may be surprised. We will go to great lengths to stop the harsh reality of adulting from hurting our offspring.

Ron Lieber reminds us, however, that "we are in the grownup-making business." He says that we need to tell our kids that we want them to have what they need, but not so much that they don't have to make a lot of really hard choices and trade-offs. Because, Lieber says, "that's what grownups do."

That doesn't mean things don't get complicated. Some things to think about: How would you handle it if you knew your child was putting off a medical procedure because they had a big deductible and were saving for goals you agreed were important? Would you step in and offer to pay the out-of-pocket medical costs for your child? That way they can stay on track with the goal you really want them to reach. And yes, I'm looking in the mirror as I write this. We have paid for an out-of-network second opinion for our adult daughter when she had a potentially serious medical issue. We weren't going to let a financial lesson stand in the way of her health. But we were also no longer supporting her everyday expenses and had the resources. Parents can increase their own financial strength by stepping back and letting our kids function as adults – and then have the resources available for when money really can solve important problems.

I bring this up to illustrate that many of these choices aren't about bratty kids asking for parents to pay for the latest iPhone when they are 25 years old. Many young adults have high deductible health plans and do put off medical appointments. They may delay getting a car fixed, and then it breaks down and they can't afford to fix it. Without the car, they can't get to their job. You can write a check to fix this. Will you? How will you keep this from becoming a pattern?

There are real and complicated financial dilemmas that will come up. How you decide to manage them will depend on not just your financial ability to help your child in the short term but also on the long-term implications of that help. We must avoid a chronic bailout pattern.

Mixed Messages

Parents also send mixed messages. I know I do all the time. I once scolded my stepdaughter for spending money on taxis because every charge takes away from her long-term goal of saving for a home down payment. Minutes later I suggested she consider getting a share house in the Hamptons over the summer. That, of, course would have been monumentally more expensive. I was a total hypocrite. She was quick to call me out on it.

And while we are looking in the mirror, over the years I have had the privilege of knowing that my financially stable parents would be there as a backstop for me. But somehow, my mom and dad were able to balance making sure I knew they would be there in a true financial emergency with making sure I never wanted to be in a position to need their emergency support.

That is the real sweet spot we should all try to be at as parents.

For most of us, it's a struggle to find that balance. For example, we tell our children to save as much as possible. Put that earned income in a Roth IRA before you have other responsibilities of being an adult, like children of your own. We want them to get that compound interest going as fast as possible with as much money as possible. We also want them to feel rewarded for their work and excited to have their own spending money. So we want to be cool with letting them have some fun with the money they earned. They will probably be at this amazing semi-carefree time of their life only once. They are old enough to do big things and have some financial resources but in most cases aren't weighed down by some of the more costly adult realities like children of their own.

To Subsidize or Not to Subsidize?

We want to teach our kids not to spend more than they can afford and stay on track to reach their financial goals. But what if their friends are going to a destination wedding, or a spa weekend, concert or sports event to celebrate a big birthday, and the cost of that is above what they can afford? These are milestone life experiences that you do not want them to miss out on because they want to hit the max in their Roth IRA. What about after college when work colleagues are going out for pricey drinks? That's not just fun; that's networking. If they aren't getting to know colleagues, they could miss out on important career relationships that can lead to meaningful opportunities. It is an investment in their future.

Let's get real. Very few parents are going to tell their child not to spend their money on those kinds of things. And if we are being honest, some of us will even subsidize them. That can be okay – just not forever and not taken for granted. There has to be an understanding that the help is temporary and has a specific timeline.

On a practical level, our children might not be rushing out to get their first job as soon as they're old enough – in high school or even before – unless they get to spend at least some of the money however they want. They want financial freedom. And for most kids, they will want to spend it. What feels more grownup than walking into a store like a boss and walking out with something you pay for with money you personally earned?

Here's where it can get interesting. You may not want them to pay their own bills. It may make sense, especially if you subscribe to the concept of a family ecosystem, for you to continue to subsidize some bills, so they can allocate resources to goals that will create a foundation for adult financial independence. For example, you may prefer that they put their earned income into a Roth IRA, as I did with my teenagers. Or for them to save for college. Maybe you want them to build up an emergency savings fund so they can live independently after graduation? Or just let them make their own choices and use whatever happens as a foundation for teaching them about money. Sometimes it's a good thing to let them make mistakes. They may surprise you and make some great choices – even if that comes after some really bad choices. Kids are often savvier than we expect when we give them a little wiggle room.

Another consideration: Not all bills are created equal. You might want them to pay for activities with their friends with their money at age 16 but still cover their phone bill, especially if they are on a family plan and it is very small. And do you really want your kids to reimburse you for their health insurance while they are in high school even if they have income? It's your call.

For teens, the goal is usually to get them to pay enough to appreciate and learn the relative costs of things. Using the phone as an example, maybe they can pay for the extra data bandwidth they insist on so they can watch a ton of videos on YouTube. Or for the device upgrade when the phone they already have is just fine in your opinion but all their friends have the latest model. You can still pay for the basic plan. Once they are out of school and in a full-time job, it will probably make sense to adjust the rules. At that point, the goal is to offload as much as possible without being penny-wise pound foolish.

Financial psychologist and CERTIFIED FINANCIAL PLANNER™ professional Brad Klontz says, "Are they behaving like responsible adults in every other aspect of their lives, except that you are paying for Netflix? I wouldn't worry about that so much. However, is there a pattern of them being less responsible, and taking less initiative, because at the back of their mind they have a money script that says there will always be enough money?" Consider putting expenses into three mindsets:

Keep it in the family ecosystem. Applying the financial grownup mindset of common sense and generosity, it doesn't make sense to create an additional cost, just to prove a point.

Financial grownup time. These are money-related milestones and times when they need to step up and own the expense as financial grownups.

It's complicated. There are times when a parent can make a financial move into adulthood a lot easier, but there are varying benefits and consequences. But because the child could likely manage themselves if they had to, it's not always clear what is the best way to proceed. Decisions often come down to the personalities involved and the relationship between everyone.

Here are some examples of expenses your child can take over and how the different mindsets can be applied.

Credit Cards

Keep it in the family ecosystem. Some premium cards offer benefits to the entire family at little or no additional costs. For example, the American Express Platinum allows up to three authorized users on a card for an additional $175. If you are already paying that for one or two users, keeping an adult child as the third authorized user can give them access to economical perks like free airport lounge access, which can save money on food and drinks when traveling.

Financial grownup time. If they don't already have their own credit card, they should get one now. Getting a no-fee credit card that they pay off each month will not only teach them to manage their cash flow but also help establish a credit history that will allow them access to other adult privileges like being able to get a mortgage or car loan. They should also consider sign up bonuses and choosing cards that have rewards and bonuses in places they use frequently.

It's complicated. If they aren't yet on their own credit card, you may have to help them out. One option is to cosign. The problem is that leaves the parent vulnerable. You are responsible for their debt if they don't pay it. It can also negatively impact your own credit score. Another option is a secured card. It is backed by a cash deposit, which is often equal to the credit limit. This is also better for building credit than a prepaid debit card.

One more thing: Keeping them on plans as authorized users doesn't mean they have to actually use the cards at all, so you can set a low limit on their use and have it there for emergencies only. Be sure to regularly check your bills, and make sure they pay you back for anything they charge. Trust but verify.

Discretionary, Entertainment, Dining Out

Keep it in the family ecosystem. If you are at a family gathering, the truth is, if it is affordable, it is nice for the parents to pay. Especially if there are younger siblings present, singling out an older child and presenting them with their share of the bill may be a bit much.

Financial grownup time. Anytime they are spending money that is for them. This can be going out with their friends, buying their own food, and shopping in general. You may choose to buy them an outfit for the first day of work, but in general spending on clothing should be on them.

It's complicated. If a child is living at home, separating out food and having an adult-age child paying for their own everyday groceries can sometimes get complicated. Do you really want to start labeling whose food it is, especially if other siblings are around? You are a family, not roommates. The big exception: if they order delivery for themselves, it is on them. Same thing with ordering on-demand movies.

One more thing: Content subscriptions like Netflix and Hulu. If you are paying for a family plan, the truth is your child can log in at no additional cost even if they don't live at home. So it generally doesn't make sense to knock them off. This goes to common sense.

Health Insurance

The best news in recent years is that this is actually a choice. Kids can stay on their parents plans until age 26.

Keep it in the family ecosystem. If the parents' plan is priced in a way that there is no incremental additional cost per child, the children should stay until age 26 regardless of whether they have insurance available at their job unless their employer pays all the costs and it is a better plan. If the premium is literally not costing you more, there is no real cost to pass on. One caveat: make sure the coverage is the same. Some plans offer lesser coverage to dependents than to the primary insured person.

Financial grownup time. Adult children should pay their copays and any other costs that are not covered. They should be responsible for filing the forms themselves and keeping track of their own balances and deductibles so they learn how health insurance works. Bills should be addressed to them, even if they still live at home.

It's complicated. If the parents' plan is priced per dependent, it may or may not be more expensive than the plan offered by their employer. Also, employer options may be a far better fit for the child. For example, your child could be offered a high deductible health plan that comes with a cash contribution from the company. According to the Employee Benefits Research Institute (EBRI) the average company contribution to an individual employee's health savings account in 2020 was $864.[1] If a child is healthy and expected to only use the wellness visits, that free money may be worth considering. And as a reminder, HSAs avoid taxes both when contributions are made and if used as intended when contributions come out of the plan. That makes it one of the best savings vehicles out there.

Also key: While adult children can stay on *medical* plans until they turn 26, the same does not hold true for dental or eyewear plans. They may end earlier, often at age 23. Be sure to check so you are not caught off-guard if your child stays on your plan.

One more thing: Timing is also important. If the job starts late in the plan cycle year, the child's deductible on the parents' plan may already be met, and it might make sense to delay the switch over until the next open enrollment. That's what we did. Once they are paying for their own health care, kids will learn very quickly that there are strong financial incentives to go to doctors in network and to look for ways to lower costs. We witnessed this in our own family. For example, many prescription drug companies now offer coupons for prescriptions right on their websites. You just have to look. A kid who previously might not have bothered will get very good at this very fast once they are paying for their own health care.

Phone Plans

Keep it in the family ecosystem. Every plan differs, but in most cases the cost of an individual plan is going to be higher than the incremental cost of keeping an employed adult child on a family plan. Parents may also be on a legacy plan and be grandfathered into an unlimited plan. That makes it an easy decision if you do the math compared with a brand-new individual plan with that carrier. Employed adult kids can still contribute their share of the family plan. They may see things differently and choose to lower their data plan and other features when they realize they have to cover the additional costs. Have them set this up as an autopay so that you are not asking them for money every month.

Financial grownup time. If your child has a job where the employer is covering part or all of the expense, they most likely must be on a separate plan from the family to get that benefit. Also, the child is potentially getting a corporate rate, which may be even better than staying on your family plan.

It's complicated. It pays to check around because opening up a new plan, even an individual one, can often come with incentives if you switch carriers, and the math may change. If it costs less to stay on the family plan, young adults should contribute at least part of their share so that they get used to the cost and include it in their budgets.

Car and Transportation-Related Costs

Keep it in the family ecosystem. If a child is a dependent living at home and driving their parent's car, it will likely be less expensive to keep them on the insurance plan, but the child should still pay their share of the premium. Should they need to file a claim, the child should also cover the deductible and any other bills. And yes, the same goes for gasoline, parking costs, any tickets they may get, or other costs to using the car.

Financial grownup time. If the car is in the child's name, they most likely need to have their own insurance. Also, car insurance premiums can vary dramatically state to state in the United States. A child may move to a state with lower insurance rates.

It's complicated. Keeping young adults, who are considered riskier and therefore charged more for insurance than their older counterparts, on the plan is disproportionately more expensive than other shared family costs. By removing them, parents' premiums will often decrease dramatically – as will premiums for added protections like umbrella insurance. It may come down to your own financial needs more than anything else. Run the numbers.

One more thing: Make sure your child is eligible to stay on your insurance. If the insurance requires that they be a dependent, confirm that they meet the requirements, or you may find them not covered should you need to file a claim.

Get Everyone Onboard

For all of these, the most important thing, as always, is to make sure all of this is communicated to your kids in a loving but firm way. You may even want to write them down so there are no misunderstandings and you start to see accidental charges on your credit card. If you are married or have a partner who is co-parenting, make sure they are fully onboard, so you don't send mixed messages or undermine each other.

And when you have doubts and want to rescue them, take Task's words of wisdom to heart: "You are taking away their opportunity to grow. They need to fly on their own. You are literally clipping their wings because you are being selfish because you enjoy giving."

Review

1. Adult children should pay for their regular personal bills as soon as they have a full-time job.
2. Parents can treat children to things that are discretionary such as meals, family trips, and use of subscriptions like Netflix, as long as it is well within the parents' own financial budgets.
3. Don't create new expenses to make a point. If it is less expensive for the overall family to consolidate bills, as with mobile phones or car insurance, do so. The young adult child can pay their share.
4. Make sure the child is aware that while they can stay on medical insurance until age 26, dental and eye coverage often end at 23 or earlier. If a plan is available at their job and is either the same cost or less expensive, they should switch to that plan.
5. Be strategic and stay on top of what's going on with credit cards. Make sure your kids have their own to improve their credit score, but keep them on premium ones that carry cash savings benefits like airport lounges, even if they do not use them for spending.

CHAPTER 9

Paycheck 101

I had a text exchange with my son.
He said, "Hey mom, you know what's great?"
And I said, "What?"
He said, "Getting paid."
And then he wrote, "You know what sucks?"
And I said, "What?"
He said, "Taxes."
And he sent me a picture!
—Jean Chatzky, founder and CEO, HerMoney.com
and host of the HerMoney podcast

They Got Paid! Helping Your Child Understand Their First Paycheck

Earlier we heard about my own child's visceral response to her first adult paycheck. Opening that first paycheck is exciting but also often a tough reality check for our children learning how income works in the grownup world. Odds are their net income is a lot less than the pay they expected to receive. It is also a lesson in how a good part of where our earnings go is out of our control. As U.S. citizens, we have to pay taxes. There are choices we can make that can help us pay less, but most of us will pay more than we would like. The first paycheck will also provide an opportunity to you as a parent to talk about the upside of maximizing the programs young adults have access to if they work for a corporation that offers retirement and other benefits and strategies to help with tax planning.

After giving them a little emotional support and agreeing that yes, it is totally not fair that so little is left after all the things are taken out, it is essential that we as parents go through the paycheck line by line and help them understand where their earnings are going. While you are at it, you can double-check that they are taking out money for things they should. That likely includes a retirement plan such as a 401(k), disability insurance, possibly commuter benefits if that is an option, and of course the right amount of tax withholding.

Many of us have had decades of paychecks so feel free to skip to the next chapter at this point. But for those of us, including myself, who sometimes need a refresher, here are some of the most common things your child will see on their paystub if they work for a corporation. We'll go into more detail on how benefits work in the next chapter.

Employee Identifying Information

The top section will usually include their name, their social security number, employee ID, address, and other identifying information, as well as a check number. Make sure your child checks that these are all accurate right from the start. A typo on something like their Social Security number could cause a lot of headaches in the future!

Pay Period

This may not seem significant, but it is worth noting how our children's paychecks are scheduled. For example, some paychecks come out twice a month, which works out to 24 paychecks per year. Some paychecks are every two weeks, which means about 26 paychecks a year and thus a lower amount per paycheck. They should also note the date of deposit. Some companies pay employees a bit ahead and some a bit in arrears. This isn't something your child can control, but it is something they should be aware of and understand.

HOURS WORKED   Many companies will have this in your child's paycheck even if they are not paid on an hourly basis. In that case, it will appear the same on every paycheck. It is worth noting because it can be confusing to a new-ish worker who receives a set salary, even though for accounting purposes the company breaks their compensation down to an hourly wage. This was my experience at one of my reporting jobs and I went to HR to make sure I had been placed in the correct pay band and my job classification was correct. Mistakes do get made so if you have any concerns, have your child confirm everything was put into the system correctly.

OVERTIME HOURS   If your child received pay for overtime, that will appear separately. If they are different categories, such as standard overtime and holiday pay, they will often be broken out into separate lines as well. Let them know that when they have a surge in overtime, their tax withholding may change, but that it will be adjusted when they file their taxes.

BONUS PAY   This may be labeled differently but can include spot bonuses or annual bonuses, etc. Let your child know that, as with overtime, this kind of pay may have taxes withheld at a higher rate but that it will be adjusted when they do their taxes.

HOLIDAY OR PAID TIME OFF (PTO) PAY   Many companies break this out. As your child uses up their time off, that is calculated separately. It can be useful to see how much their time is actually worth, and if they have unused time off, it could be money your child can collect when they leave the company.

Note: other types of absences from work such as family leave, sick days, and even bereavement days may be broken out separately.

REIMBURSEMENTS   This is important to note for your child because they may have out-of-pocket expenses they need to file with their employer, especially if they travel. They will often show up in the paystub. Make sure they know how to file expenses and to follow up to make sure the re-imbursement shows up in a timely manner.

Gross Wages

This is simply how much money was earned for that pay period before any deductions.

YTD Gross Wages

This is the sum total of how much money they have earned year-to-date.

Net Pay

We like to call this take-home pay. It is the amount of money left after all the deductions including taxes and elective withholding. This number is what usually triggers that primal scream we talked about earlier.

Pretax Deductions

These are items that will lower your child's tax bill – although in some cases like retirement accounts, taxes will be due in the future.

HEALTH INSURANCE   This is the share of the premium that your child will pay for their health insurance coverage. In most cases the employer is paying a substantial portion of the premium as well. Make sure they understand how the plan works and that they confirm their enrollment at each year's open enrollment period unless they have other insurance.

DENTAL INSURANCE   Not all companies offer dental, but when they do it can be paid pretax.

VISION INSURANCE   Vision is also not always offered but if available can be a pretax payment. It usually offers discounts on eyewear and contact lenses at major retailers but some plans also now offer discounts on procedures like Lasik.

PRETAX RETIREMENT PLAN CONTRIBUTIONS SUCH AS A 401(K)   This is where they can see what they are contributing. There may be a separate line for the company's contributions if there is a matching program in a different section. Most likely the 401(k) company match is on a vesting schedule and if your child leaves this job before being fully vested, they will forfeit that money.

GROUP LIFE INSURANCE   Some companies offer life insurance plans that can be paid for with pretax money, but the tax code is complicated here. In general, if it is a free or very low-cost benefit it is worth having but is likely not enough coverage.

Note: Your child may be able to purchase additional life insurance and disability insurance for themselves or for a dependent with after-tax money as a benefit offered by their employer.

ACCIDENTAL DEATH AND DISMEMBERMENT INSURANCE   This is also sometimes offered by an employer and can be paid with pretax earnings. AD&D Insurance is a bit morbid but essentially it covers things that happen tied to an accident. That could be a fatality but also things like paralysis, losing speech, hearing, sight, or a limb.

This is different from workers compensation insurance, which only covers applies to work-related accidents.

If the premium is paid by the employer, the benefit will be tax-free, if it is paid in a lump sum payment.

HEALTH SAVINGS PLAN (HSA)   This is available to your child if they have a high deductible health plan. The money put into this account – even from their employer – is vested right away, and will remain theirs even if they leave the job. It is not "use it or lose it" like the flexible spending account (coming up next!).

The money in the HSA can be used for medical expenses at any time, or can be saved and invested to become a defacto retirement plan. It is important that young adults stay on top of the money as it accumulates and make periodic decisions on whether to move part of the money into investments.

FLEXIBLE SPENDING PLAN   This is available if your child is not in a high deductible health plan; whatever money is put into the account must be spent during the calendar year beginning January 1 and ending December 31. Recently, some companies have added grace periods to that deadline. But once the deadline passes, the money is forfeited. During open enrollment, your child will decide how much they will contribute for the next 12 months. If your child leaves their job, any unused funds go back to the employer.

COMMUTER BENEFITS   Some companies offer commuter benefits to their employees as a benefit that can be paid for with pretax money. The rules vary by state, but in many cases this money can be used to pay for public transportation or parking a car. If your child's company doesn't offer it, and they could benefit from it, it may make sense for them to suggest it to the HR department as a cost-effective way to attract and retain employees.

FEDERAL TAXES   Every paycheck, your child's employer will take out an estimated amount of money that will go to pay their federal taxes. While the goal is for your child not to owe money at tax time, it is only an estimate; they may owe more money, or they may get a refund.

FICA TAX   This stands for Federal Insurance Contributions Act. Money is withheld by your employer and is used to pay into social security. The system's primary purpose is to provide government benefits to retired and disable people.

One way to soften the blow: let your child know that their employer is actually splitting the bill with them. Both your child and their employer each contribute 6.2 percent for social security but only on the first $142,800 as of 2021. Your child's paycheck shows what they have paid. If your child is self-employed, in the gig economy, or owns their own business, they have to pay both sides.

FICA MEDICARE TAX   This comes in at an additional 1.45 percent and gets higher if your child's income climbs above certain thresholds.

STATE TAX   This will depend on where you live because not all states have an income tax.

LOCAL TAXES   Some employees, like in my home of New York City, will also pay local income taxes.

After-Tax Deductions

AFTER-TAX RETIREMENT PLANS SUCH AS A ROTH 401(K)   If your child is in a low tax bracket it may make sense to save after-tax money for retirement since the tax will likely be lower now than when they retire.

INSURANCE   Some companies will offer various kinds of insurance such as disability insurance for your child as well as their spouses and dependents if they have them, as an after-tax benefit.

529 PLANS   These allow regular contributions allocated for education. They can be invested and grow tax-free and eventually taken out to pay for education tax-free.

UNION DUES   If your child is in a union, unfortunately the dues are not deductible unless they are self-employed, in which case it would be a business expense.

The Self-Employed Child

The good news is that there are now many resources for people who are self-employed, including companies that will create a payroll-like system for freelancers or self-employed individuals. While they will not get the corporate subsidized benefits of an employee, being self-employed will allow your child many other benefits including business-related deductions.

Note: This also may apply to income from a side hustle that is also going to be taxable.

The key things for them to pay attention to include:

Taxes

They must pay taxes on a quarterly basis. They can get more information about self-employment taxes right on the IRS website at https://www.irs.gov/businesses/small-businesses-self-employed/self-employed-individuals-tax-center.

Retirement Plans

Although they won't get matching funds from an employer, being self-employed will often allow them to save more money for retirement and enjoy other benefits.

Business-Related Deductions

This will vary depending on their business. As an example of how important it is to keep track of how you spend money, consider how home office expenses have grown during the pandemic. If you worked for a company, those expenses were not a tax deduction for you as an employee. But if you were self-employed, in most cases home office expenses would be considered a tax-deductible expense.

Review

1. First paychecks can be both a celebration and a somber reality check.
2. Young adults should carefully inspect their first few paychecks for errors and for adjustments they might want to make.
3. Understanding where their earned income is going and how it is taxed will help adult children make informed decisions as they move through their careers.
4. Self-employed young adults still have to pay attention to their income throughout the year and make sure to plan for taxes, retirement plans, and potential deductions.

CHAPTER 10

Jobs with Benefits

We underestimate how much hand-holding needs to happen because we all figured it out the hard way.
—Pam Capalad, CFP®, AFP® founder, and CEO Brunch & Budget

Making the right benefit choices when it comes to a first full-time job can be the first step in a successful wealth-building strategy – or a costly delay in building the right foundation.

Parents can make a huge impact on their child's future financial success by pushing to be included in these early decisions, starting with making sure the kids are fully aware of the benefits they should be looking for – and negotiating for – even when they are looking for a job, and negotiating a job offer.

CERTIFIED FINANCIAL PLANNER™ professional Pam Capalad says parents often think their young adults are good to go based on their corporate orientation session or assume they will just read their new employer's HR section on the website. That's because most of the time that's what the kids tell us. But better to be safe than sorry years later when your young adult missed out on some huge financial benefits. "We underestimate how much hand-holding needs to happen because we all figured it out the hard way. So were like, oh, invest in a 401(k). And then they'll know the rest. I think we take for granted what the rest is."

Timing is everything with benefits, and there are generally two kinds of choices if they have a full-time staff job with a corporation: the ones that lock you in for a year, and the ones that you can change pretty much at any time. If they are self-employed, there are ways to create their own benefits package, but it is more complicated to go the DIY route and often there are additional costs to consider. We'll get to that later in the chapter.

Health Coverage

Before your child accepts a full-time position, they should make sure to confirm that health insurance will be offered. If not, they will need to factor that into their costs when they discuss compensation. We'll cover more about that in the DIY benefits section. If health insurance is offered, it pays to put the time in to make sure your young adult knows first and foremost when they can sign up. Health insurance is often available only in certain windows. In almost every case if your young adult child is offered health insurance through their job, it is going to be a better deal than getting it on the Health Insurance Marketplace® (The Marketplace) at healthcare.gov.

Some employers may require your child to be at the company for a few months before they are eligible to sign up for one of their plans. Some may require that new employees sign up within a certain window after your child begins the job. If they don't sign up during that time period, your child may not be able to sign up again until the annual open enrollment period – so it is essential that your child be aware of the rules and get that insurance if it will be needed. All may not be lost for a full year if they miss the window. They may be able to enroll if they have a qualifying event. That generally means a change in family status or some reason why they have a change in circumstances. The good news is that turning 26 and losing coverage from a parent's plan counts as a qualifying event. This could be especially meaningful if the open enrollment windows for your family's insurance and your young adult's insurance are not at the same time.

It's so important for parents to be deliberate in this decision and not just leave it up to the kid. Now that insurance companies are required to allow children up to age 26 to be on their parents' insurance, many employers will push younger employees to stay on their parents' insurance. When our daughter got her first job, her employer's HR department "assumed" she would just stay on our insurance. In fact, she told us that in orientation meetings that was the expectation from the company for the incoming class of staffers. It saves them money because companies subsidize their employees' health insurance. Make sure that is the best decision for your family and not just what is best for your child's new employer. When we did the math for our family, we realized that it was more expensive for our daughter to stay on our insurance. She signed up for her own plan, which also offered heavy incentives that would jump-start her retirement savings and investing.

If your child does stay on your plan, they can still certainly reimburse you, the parents, for a portion of the premium, and any copays or additional costs associated with their health care. If your adult child isn't living near you but will stay on your health plan, make sure the in-network doctors are near them; otherwise, you should factor in the travel costs associated with bringing them home for all their doctor's visits. Plus, if they have an emergency, they'll (and you if you're helping) likely have much higher out-of-pocket expenses.

Terms to Know

Health care lingo can be complicated. When you're helping your child choose a plan of their own, it's important to know certain nuances of each one and evaluate how these costs stack up against your child's ability to pay if and when something happens and they need care. Here's a list of terms to get you started:

- **Premium:** The amount that will automatically be deducted tax free from your child's paycheck. This might be the entire cost, but typically employers cover some to all of the premium for at least the employee.

- **Copay:** A fixed dollar amount your child will pay each time they go to a doctor, take a trip to urgent care or the ER, or get a prescription filled.
- **Deductible:** The amount your child has to spend (total sum) before their health plan begins to pay. Let's say their deductible is $500. This means that they must pay the total bill for any medical care they receive until they have spent at least $500—then their plan will start to cover care, often at a percentage based on their plan's coinsurance.
- **Coinsurance:** The percentage your child will pay after meeting any required deductible. For example, a routine surgery costing $5,500 with a plan deductible of $500 and an 80/20 coinsurance (plan pays 80 percent and child pays 20 percent) will cost your child $500 + (20 percent of $5,500 = $1,100) = $1,600.
- **Annual out-of-pocket maximum:** The most your child will have to pay *total* in a 365-day time frame (typically January 1 to December 31, but make sure your child knows what their plan's rules are). After they reach this number, their plan will cover 100 percent of all health care costs the plan covers. Note: It doesn't include costs outside of what the plan will pay for, like if your child is outside the network or gets an elective surgery or procedure that's not approved.

Savings Plans

Employers typically offer two ways to put money aside for medical costs: health savings accounts (HSAs) and flexible spending accounts (FSAs). Companies often contribute money to these as part of the benefit package they offer.

HSAs   With an HSA, with every paycheck your child can set aside tax-free money (up to a certain limit), save it indefinitely, let it earn interest, and spend it on a very generous list of health care expenses. If your child is healthy and doesn't spend any or much of it, the money spent over the years, acting as a sort of bonus retirement account. In the future, the money may even be eligible to be taken out of the account tax free.

HSAs are triple tax free and are fast becoming known as a great option to save and invest for retirement if some of the funds are not needed for medical care. And the money goes with you if you leave your job. The money is also accessible for other purposes if needed, but I don't recommend this because of taxes and penalties. Plus, taking money out defeats the whole purpose.

FSAs   Like HSAs, FSA's are funded with pre-tax money and can be used for medical-related expenses. They also have limits on how much you can set aside each year – this changes, so your child can either ask their human resources department or look on irs.gov for more information.

The main difference between the two is that FSA funds are use it or lose it – whatever you don't spend disappears at the end of each year. If you have money in there, you just lose it. So it's important to help your kids be realistic in estimating how much money they want taken out of their gross paycheck for the upcoming year. An FSA saves on taxes but doesn't earn interest; plus, the money stays with the employer if your child doesn't spend it all before their last day of work.

When you're going over the differences between an HSA and an FSA with your child, let them know that one perk of an FSA relates to when the money becomes available. Employers load all the money *for the whole year* – whatever they are going to contribute plus what your child has designated to be taken out of their paycheck – onto the card at the beginning of the year. Think of it as an advance that, if spent, they don't even have to pay back if they leave the company before the end of the year. The flipside is that if they pay in more than they spend, and leave, they lose the money they have paid in.

While it may not be relevant just yet, let your kids know one more benefit for the future when you might not be as involved: the Dependent Care FSA. This money can be used for childcare expenses which are defined by the Internal Revenue Service. An updated list can be found on IRS.gov.

Plan Types

The industry is always evolving and changing, but these are some typical health plan choices offered by employers.

HIGH DEDUCTIBLE HEALTH CARE PLANS (HDHPs) These are growing in popularity with younger workers because they are cheaper and have a ton of perks. The premiums are generally significantly lower than other plans because they have high deductibles. In other words, if your child chooses this plan, they will be on the hook for any medical costs that happen before they reach the hefty deductible. The lowest a deductible will be as of 2021 is $1400 for an individual – and it could be higher.

These high deductible plans come with the big incentive being access to an HSA. And many companies are working to encourage workers to sign up for the high deductible plans by offering major cash bonuses. Typical programs include contributing $750 or more to the employee's HSA account.

This is not taxed as income – another win. If you leave the company, this money is portable so you can take it with you. Also good: if you are self-employed and you qualify, you can have an HSA and the tax and investing benefits that go along with the program. The amount saved can be adjusted throughout the year, not just at open enrollment time.

Capalad says it is a risk–tolerance discussion. With the high deductible comes a risk that your child could have high medical bills and will have to pay for them either out of their HSA or some other source. Really think about your child's personality and likely medical needs. If they have to pay out-of-pocket every time they go to the doctor, will they go? Will you find yourself stepping in and offering to pay for the doctor just to get them to go? Do they have in-network doctors in their area, which will give them lower cost options? As much as a plan may make sense financially, it has to also work for your child's life and personality.

Here is a sample of what you as a parent could say to your child to get them thinking:

"How would you feel if you got a giant bill that you've had to pay, even though you had an HSA that you set aside money for it. Does that make you more stressed? Does that make you more nervous? Would you avoid or postpone going, in the hopes you get better?"

If your child says yes to these questions, Capalad advises telling your child to pay the higher premium, which has less out-of-pocket financial risk. Also remember that while your child will have to live with the plan they choose for a year, it is only a year, and they can switch plans at the next open enrollment period.

HMOs These plans have a *network* of doctors and hospitals you're restricted to. With an HMO, you also must always see your primary doctor (sometimes called a PCP) first; you can't just go see a specialist on your own. Your doctor has to see you first and then give you permission to see someone else. This is called a preauthorization, and if you don't do this you will likely pay for all of the cost on your own – none of it will be covered. On the upside, because this type of plan has the most restrictions, it is almost always the cheapest, and deductibles are very low to nonexistent.

PPOs These plans also have a network of doctors, but you don't have to see your primary doctor first. Plus, you can go out of the network if you want. It will cost more than an HMO but offers a lot more flexibility.

THE MARKETPLACE   If your child is not a full-time employee, is working freelance, or is starting their own business, they may want to look into ACA plans at healthcare.gov. While many plans are expensive and the system is far from perfect, having health insurance is always a good idea. And as mentioned already, an HSA is likely an option, which can soften the blow a bit. A number of plans are offered during specific enrollment periods. Because information is ever evolving, it's best to go to the website for the most updated information.

Dental Coverage

While the ACA extended coverage of medical insurance to our children up to age 26, this did not include dental insurance. Some plans of course can choose to offer coverage at older ages, but many don't. Our family plan requires adult children to roll off the plan at age 23, so our daughter has her own dental insurance. The law on this could change, so the important thing is to know what your family coverage options are and make an informed decision.

If your child has a full-time job, they might be offered dental insurance. Like medical insurance, a pretax amount will be deducted from their paycheck each month. Then it's important for you to explain that the out-of-pocket costs and coverage for dental plans are sort of opposite from their health plan. While there is often a very small deductible, after that the insurance often kicks in, covering a certain percentage of a dental service, depending on what that service is and if the dentist is in network. Typically there is no copay; most cleanings are covered at 100 percent as long as the dentist is in the plan's network. And for big procedures like fillings and crowns the patient pays a percentage of the whole cost.

But here's the catch: There are often yearly and lifetime coverage limits. For example, coverage per year in a typical plan might end after your child is reimbursed $1,500. There is often a lifetime cap on orthodonture and an age limit per person. After that, you are responsible for everything on your own. That's why an HSA or FSA can be essential. Each policy has its unique rules so be sure you and your child read the fine print.

Vision Insurance

Vision coverage operates very differently from medical and dental insurance and can vary greatly. In general, these plans focus on offering discounts on things like glasses and contact lenses at major retailers, upgrades to eyewear like antireflective coatings and progressive lenses, and procedures like Lasik. Some may cover optometrist exams. Most vision care plans don't cover ophthalmologist exams. Those often fall instead under health insurance and may be covered only if there is a medical issue.

Plans can have huge variations and so this is one thing you want to really pull up and read at least once with your child. There may be some benefits in there they don't consider that they can use including prescription sunglasses.

Life Insurance

Many companies will offer a modest amount of life insurance, as a no-cost to the employee benefit.

If the company offers life insurance but requires the employee, your child, to pay for some or all of it, the premium will usually be small and well worth it. One thing to check is whether it can be carried with your child if they leave the company or if they have to get a replacement policy that could be more expensive. It will still likely be worth it, but that information will influence whether you want to buy additional independent life insurance in addition to the company offerings.

Disability Insurance

I can't stress enough how important this is. Think of it this way: at a young age, your child may not yet have large material assets like a home to protect. Odds are their greatest asset in their twenties is their ability to work and earn income. They need to protect that with disability insurance.

Disability insurance will pay a percentage of your salary if you are disabled and can't work. Many people assume this applies only to what they perceive as serious illness. But things like carpal tunnel syndrome, a back injury, or arthritis can creep up and make it impossible to work.

There are two types of disability insurance. *Short-term* disability may take a few weeks or a month to kick in and can last up to about a year depending on the plan. Some employers pay for or subsidize this, so it is essential that your young adult find out and take advantage of any benefits tied to this. As the name suggests, *long-term* disability starts when the disability is for an extended period of time. The waiting time depends on the policy, as does how long the coverage will last and which disabilities are covered by the policy. That's why it is essential that both you and your young adult read all policies carefully.

If their job does not offer disability insurance or they work for themselves, your child can buy insurance through an industry group or independently. An example of an industry group would be the Freelancers Union.[1] One way to reduce the cost of a disability policy is to increase the elimination period, or the length of time they are disabled before they can collect money. The longer the elimination period, the lower the cost. It's kind of like having a higher deductible for health insurance.

Another consideration is "Own Occupation" insurance which will pay out if they can't work in their current occupation. There is also "Residual Disability" coverage which can kick in if you can do your job, but only partially. For example, if your child is recovering from a medical procedure and can only work limited hours as they recover.

If your child's employer pays the premiums on their disability policy and they use it, they will owe taxes on that money paid out as a benefit. If they pay the premiums on the disability policy, they won't pay taxes on the money they receive as a benefit. The benefit amount (what percentage of their salary will be replaced) as well as whether the policy will be adjusted to reflect inflation also can be adjusted to control the price and make it more affordable.

Mental Health Resources

Mental health is usually included in employer benefits, but additional resources such as support groups may be available as well.

According to the SHRM 2020 benefits survey, 25 percent of respondents said their companies increased mental health benefits. Not surprisingly, Covid-19 is cited as a reason with the increased report saying "The expansion of Mental Health services may have resulted from employers recognizing the acute need to support their employees under increased stress, both work- and non-work related."

It is increasingly likely that your child's company offers Employee Assistance Programs (EAP) for mental health and wellness support.

Companies have also expanded the availability of telemedicine as a benefit. In fact that same 2020 SHRM report showed 43 percent of companies increased that benefit.

I point out the increases because these are benefits many of us did not have in the past but are becoming increasingly common and valued by employees. Encourage your young adults to know what is available to them.

Health and Wellness Perks

This is where it starts to get fun! Companies were already putting more emphasis on benefits to keep employees happy and healthy, and the COVID-19 pandemic upped the ante.

Policies vary widely and are constantly changing but usually for the better. For example, some companies will reimburse $1,000 of spending on health-related activities. The list of what is included in this has been growing. Some companies might cover part of the cost of a Peloton bicycle or the monthly subscription costs to their fitness app. Gym equipment like hand weights or a yoga mat may be covered. Personal trainer sessions can often covered. Got your eye on an Apple watch? Odds are because it can be used as a fitness tool, a company with a generous wellness policy will refund you at least part of the purchase price. And yes, my husband's company is one of them and he loves his subsidized Apple watch.

Besides the cash back and directly subsidized wellness and lifestyle benefits, many large companies also participate in discount programs. An example of this is Perks at Work, which offers employee pricing on gym memberships and dozens of other things like travel, discount show tickets, technology, online classes, and much more.

Finally, some companies offer financial incentives for doing wellness-related activities like working out and going for a yearly wellness checkup with a doctor. This can sometimes even extend to being rewarded for sustainability and environmental efforts like community service and recycling.

Commuter Benefits

Your young adults might be tempted to pass this over because it will appear as yet one more thing that will reduce their take-home pay. If they are commuting via public transportation or paying to park at or near their workplace, it is a great benefit to consider because the money taken out of their paycheck will be tax-free and ultimately cost them less. Also, if they find they are not using the benefits in most cases they can change their status with only a month's notice – unlike the restrictive once-a-year open enrollment periods of health insurance.

Legal Services

This is one that I did not use until a few years ago, and I think that was a missed opportunity. These are generally in the once-a-year category, so if your child does not sign up right away, they may have to wait until the next open enrollment period. The cost is usually very affordable and can cover a number of grownup stuff they will need legal help to get done using a defined network of lawyers. Think of it like an HMO but with lawyers. My husband and I used a lawyer in the network to create new wills.

Legal benefits may also be used for buying and selling a home, a family legal issue, dealing with debt, prenups, divorce, and even traffic violations. Every plan will vary in cost and which legal services are included, so it is essential that your young adult know what is included so they can decide if the benefit is of value to them for the coming year. For example, if they expect to buy a home, and the policy will cover the legal work associated with that, it might be worth doing for that year, and then dropping. If they don't yet have a will, they can do it that same year before dropping the plan for the next year.

You might want to use this benefit as an example of how needs change as we all go through life stages and benefits can be adjusted. Benefits are not set it and forget it – they should generally be re-assessed at least once a year.

Paid Time Off

Corporate culture plays a big part in how employees use their time off, but there is a growing recognition of the value of taking time away from work. Take a moment with your child to look at their compensation page on the HR website and see the time off allocation – and possibly its "value." Some companies even break out the time off by the hour so you can see how much it is worth in hourly wages, so your child can see the monetary value. By doing this together, you have the opportunity to share that their work has quantifiable value and also that using their PTO will positively impact their well-being. Taking time off to recharge is a habit worth forming early on.

Education and Career Development

Does your kid have their eye on graduate school or a specialized higher educational program? This may be one of the most important perks out there these days considering the ridiculous cost of higher education (speaking as a fully biased parent paying said tuition). According to the International

Foundation of Employee Benefit Plans (IFEBP), 92 percent of U.S. organizations offer some kind of educational benefit to their employees.[2]

I get really excited about this benefit because it changed my life. I learned a lot on the job as a news associate in my first post-college job at CNBC. But I also got free tuition from the company to attend NYU on the weekends for a couple of years where I took the courses required to become a CERTIFIED FINANCIAL PLANNER® practitioner. Even if I could have paid for those courses on my starting salary of $20,000, I would not have thought of it. A coworker told me about the benefit, and it seemed too good to pass up. Honestly, when you are single and don't have dependents, education that will further your career is a hobby worth encouraging.

It might take some research to learn the rules around employer-paid tuition. For example, one of my former employers offered an educational benefit, but it was not promoted. Instead, employees had to ask HR, make their case, and get manager approval. The reimbursement percentage was tied to the final grade in each course. There was also a requirement to stay at the company a certain at the company a certain length of time after completing the course. It is always worth asking about because even if there is not an official educational reimbursement policy, companies often have money budgeted for staff development that could be reallocated for tuition.

There is also a nice tax benefit. As of 2021, your child will not have to pay taxes on the first $5,250 of educational benefits used for things like tuition, fees, books, and some supplies. Be aware that some costs like meals and housing are not tax-free and unlikely to be covered by your employer. By the way, companies also get that same $5,250 tax deduction, so feel free to have your child use that information if they are trying to convince their boss of the benefits. Recent legislation has secured this until 2025; anything above that will count as income for tax purposes.

Popular opportunities can include having an employer pay for a full graduate degree like an MBA or offering their own courses to help your child advance at that company or in their chosen field. In almost every case the course of study will need to be relevant to their profession. Many companies also offer benefits to part-time employees, so don't assume there isn't money there for the asking.

Student Debt Repayment

Yes, this actually happens and in fact is snowballing in popularity. The number of employers providing direct student loan repayment as a benefit has doubled since 2018 – from 4 percent to 8 percent, according to the Society for Human Resource Management. The reason it is a growing perk is that more and more companies are competing for young workers, and one way to lure them in is the promise of helping with their student loans. According to HR consultancy Buck, 41 percent of employers said that student loan debt was a top motivator for their financial wellness offerings.[3] That is up from 23 percent in 2017.

Like everything, plans vary, and there is a range. In general, the programs I've seen offer a few thousand dollars a year and often max out at either a dollar amount or a number of years. This is free money and well worth the time to make sure your child signs up and provides the necessary documentation to get this benefit.

Coaching

It's no secret that there has been a lot of employee burnout in the last couple of years. Companies have a huge financial stake in keeping their workers feeling supported for the long term. According to the 2020 SHRM Employee Benefits survey, "Employee benefits will likely play a stronger-than-ever role in attracting talent to organizations, as organizations experience a 2021 'turnover tsunami,' with more U.S. workers quitting their jobs than at any time in at least two decades."[4] That has many companies looking beyond their internal capabilities to third party resources to offer benefits like coaching that can support employees lives beyond their day-to-day work at the company. The coaching can be financial, health, and other lifestyle support areas. The benefit may be offered as a subsidized benefit or a free benefit and is worth looking into as an added perk.

Emergency Childcare

Becoming a grandparent can be wonderful, but that does not mean you want to be the one and only backup childcare option. In fact, if you don't live nearby or are still working a 9-to-5 job, that's not even an option. That's why even if you are not yet a grandparent, it's wise to make sure your child knows whether their company offers this benefit and has a general sense of how it works. Trust me, if they become a parent, this will matter a lot.

Product Discounts

This will vary depending on the industry, but most companies love to shower their employees with free or heavily discount product samples.

I remember when my sister worked for a cookie manufacturer, her home was always filled with sweet treats that were often not yet on the market. For a company like Ben & Jerry's, that can mean a lot of free ice cream. For hospitality companies like Airbnb, your child could get travel credits. Burton offers season ski passes and snow days off. Whether your child's company offers something or not, make sure they know what's available for them and they take full advantage of this fun perk!

Donation Matching

Who doesn't love having their charitable donations go that much further? Most likely your child will be hit up to donate to everything from their college to their friends' pet projects. This is, again, one of those not secret benefits that is often overlooked. Sadly, an estimated $4–7 billion in matching gift funds goes unclaimed each year, according to Double the Donation. Each program will have its unique properties, but most charities, including schools, will be very good at helping your child get that corporate match.

Your child may feel like their donation is too small to qualify, but they should check. For example, according to Double the Donation, 93 percent of companies require the donor to give less than or equal to $50. The average minimum match amount is just $34.[5] So, if your child gives $50, their impact will actually be gifting $100. And as a reminder, if they itemize their taxes or with certain special provisions, the donation may also be tax deductible.

The vast majority – 85 percent – also offer volunteer grant programs to encourage employees to volunteer in their communities. That means that if employees volunteer at a charity for a certain number of hours, their employer will make a monetary donation as well. This is free money for the nonprofit that is often overlooked according to Double the Donation.[6] It's also a great way for your young adult child to gift to the community without using any of their own cash if that is not an option in their current budget. The key thing is that when your child volunteers they must make sure it is properly reported in their employers system so their volunteer work also brings in a donation to the charity.

This is separate from companies allowing workers to take days off to volunteer, without using any of their paid time off, which is also a common benefit they should be sure to use.

Pet Insurance

As the number of fur babies grows among young employees, expect this benefit to grow in popularity. The North American Pet Health Insurance Association (NAPHIA) 2021 State of the Industry Report shows the total number of pets insured in 2020 reached 3.1 million, up from 2.5 million the previous year. By the end of 2020, pet insurance had been growing at an average annual rate of almost 25 percent for the past 5 years.[7] Average annual premiums can be expensive: according to NAPHIA, close to $600 annually for a dog for accident and illness. So if their company offers a sub-sidized option, it is worth considering.

Pet insurance works in many ways like human insurance in that you pay a monthly premium and there is a deductible. If your pet gets sick, benefits will kick in after the deductible. Some plans have annual deductibles and have per-incident deductibles. One key difference is that most plans while others do not cover routine check ups. So make sure your young adult knows what their specific policy covers.

Free Premium Event Tickets

This is often an under-the-radar benefit that can be huge if your child knows where to look. Companies often have premium seats for top executives to entertain clients. The reality is that these tickets sometimes go unused.

This is something to ask your HR rep about informally because it may not be anywhere official but could be something occasionally posted on company message boards at the last minute. Tell your child that as they settle into the new job, to try to find out where to look, or who is the keeper of these kinds of tickets so they can be on their radar when they are up for grabs and otherwise going to waste.

Retirement

There are an alphabet soup's worth of possible retirement plans an employer can offer, so we're just going to cover the most common ones here. Many of them will work in similar ways with a few unique features.

401(k)

This is an easy yes because in most cases the company will offer a matching benefit – so free money. Just be aware of how much that free money is and when it will be paid. There are often vesting schedules, so your child should understand that they may not get all or part of the matching money for a number of years. That is something that should be very clear on the company internal employee benefits website.

I still remember the HR person at my first job at CNBC telling me that she was marking the box to have me contribute to my 401(k) before I had any idea what that was. It was so easy for my colleagues to just not bother to read what it was and not check the box – figuring they'd go look at it another time when they could afford it. That's why some companies will automatically enroll new employees and defer at least a small percentage of their pay.

I'd like you to consider two approaches to deciding how much a young worker should put aside. The first is that it should be no less than the amount the company will match. So, for example, my first job at CNBC offered a dollar for dollar match up to 6 percent of my gross pay. If your child resists – and there's a good chance they will – remind them that in a traditional 401(k) the money can be taken out of their paycheck pretax. This will lower their gross income, which will matter to them when tax season rolls around. You might also remind them of the power of compounding, which we will cover in the chapter on investing. The other approach is more aggressive and frankly a little bit aspirational – but worth discussing. Take the maximum allowed amount, which in 2021 is $19,500, and divide it by the number of paychecks. Then run the numbers and see what impact it will have on their take-home pay and ability to pay their bills. Odds are in a first job that is not going to be a realistic option, but after they have that mapped out, help them work backward to see what they can afford. Remind your child that the amount taken out of their paycheck for their 401(k) can be adjusted throughout the year – not just annually.

Many companies also offer a feature that will automatically increase the percentage taken out of a paycheck. Have your child set it up and see if they even notice. Again, they can always go back to the more comfortable number.

Traditional vs. Roth

This is a relatively new option and one that is amazing for young people. In short, a traditional 401(k) or individual retirement account (IRA) is funded with money before you pay tax. The Roth versions of these accounts are funded with money that has already been taxed. Either way they pay tax; it is just a question of when: now, when their income is probably lower than it will be in the future; or at retirement, when they might be in a higher tax bracket. There are also income and contribution limits. There are more restrictions on traditional retirement accounts; for example, a Roth account will allow your child to access some funds without penalties if they are used for certain things like a down payment for first home.

Don't stop there. Please make sure your young adult knows that these investment vehicles are just buckets and that the money must be invested in something – usually mutual funds that they select. As I shared before, regarding Ashley, it is not uncommon for people to save money but not invest it. Years can go by on auto pilot with no one the wiser, and the financial lost opportunity can be devastating when the mistake is revealed. Capalad has seen the disastrous consequences: "I've seen 30-year-olds putting money into a 401(k) for 10 years and it's not invested at all. It's just in the 401(k) savings. I've seen it with like 40- and 50-year-olds, too. They just had no idea."

This is heartbreaking because the consequences will be unfixable, and it would have been so easy to prevent. Capalad's clients come to her and say they were doing the thing they were told to do: put money into a 401(k). But no one explained to them that it is supposed to hold investments that you need to choose. She does point out that now some plans will autoinvest the money into target date funds. But that is still not always the case.

The DIY Benefits Plan

I'm not going to sugarcoat it: this is not easy and will require work beyond this book. The transition from dependent child to not-financially-dependent young adult goes a lot smoother with an employer providing some of the perks and safety nets we have outlined so far in this chapter.

That said, either by choice or by default, many young adults who are working as freelancers, as contractors, for small businesses, or for themselves will not have corporate benefits as they emerge into adulthood. It will be tough to match what bigger companies can offer. But the most essential things like health insurance and long-term saving and investing can be created for an individual – though it's more work and in many cases more costly.

The good news is that young adults can remain on their parents' health insurance until they are 26 years old. That buys a nice chunk of time to figure things out. After that, they can buy it on the Marketplace or through various trade groups and unions.

Retirement planning, however, should not be delayed until age 26. Jean Chatzky took a proactive approach in helping her son set up his own retirement investing plan. In his first few jobs, he had worked as a contractor or long-term temporary employee and did not have a company retirement plan. She showed him how to open a Roth IRA in a robo-advisor account, along with automatic monthly contributions. "He called me a couple of years later. And he was just like, 'Why didn't I do this sooner?'"

Using a robo-advisor took the pressure off her son having to pick stocks. He was able to let the app set up and manage the portfolio. Chatzky says he was so excited watching his money grow. "His balance is significantly more than his contributions. I mean, he was fortunate enough to start doing this in the midst of a bull market."

Work Culture: Best Behavior and Making Good Choices

First jobs can be a shock to the system, especially for young adults whose primary experience with adult authority has been limited to their parents and teachers. While our homes may not be full-on democracies, we as parents often do take their happiness into account when we make decisions. Most of all, we have an emotional attachment to the kids. We also can't fire our kids.

Employers also want our kids to succeed but it is more complicated. They are being paid, and with that pay comes expectations and consequences. While a boss might have empathy for the reason a deadline is missed or give them a pass for being late to a meeting, that will last only so long.

You Are Not the Boss of You at Work

. . . And you may not like the person who is. One of the toughest adjustments for young people is that we can choose our friends but generally can't choose our coworkers or our boss. Yet these people will have an outsize impact on how successful we are in our careers. Your child will spend a ton of time with this person and will have to participate in managing this relationship. Make sure they understand the stakes involved and that they need to be acutely aware of the authority their boss has.

You may be rolling your eyes at this, but young adults who have been accommodated through much of their lives to this point can get overwhelmed and even crushed by a boss who throws work at them at all hours and in great amounts. To some degree, they may have to step up. Obviously, if this were to rise to an abusive level, that's a different story. But in some fields – especially high-paying ones like finance and technology – young workers get piles of work and are expected to be on call all the time. Make sure your child knows what they are getting into and knows where to go for support if it gets to be too much.

Showing Up Really Is Half the Battle

CERTIFIED FINANCIAL PLANNER™ professional Liz Weston of NerdWallet says you are there to please either the boss or the client. "That's something that people don't think to teach their kids necessarily. Showing up whether you feel like it or not, pleasing the boss, or going the extra mile. That the words 'that's not in my job description' should never pass your lips."

Be present. Even if your child is working remotely, it is important that they make themselves available. Yes, they deserve to have a life. But if they want to succeed in a job where someone is paying them, or with a business where a client is paying them, it will be to their benefit to communicate that they prioritize their job and care about their success.

Dress the Part

This has become a tough one given all the changes going on in the workplace. Almost every kind of job and business is experiencing changes in how we are expected to present ourselves when working. However the expectations evolve, how we present ourselves at work matters, and it is important for us to make sure our young adults are clued in.

Just this week my husband took a Zoom call in his pajamas. Granted, the top looked like a madras shirt – but still. It is a bit of the Wild West out there. One popular strategy is to aspire to dress like your best-dressed peer or someone slightly above you at the workplace. I have often been advised to dress for the job you want, not the one you have.

When your child starts their job, it may be hard to instantly have that work wardrobe. They might have a little more wiggle room if they are working from home either full or part time. But eventually they will probably have to face coworkers or clients in person. By the way, not only is there nothing wrong with buying your child a few outfits for their first job – it's a great adulting milestone ritual to share. So go for it!

Review

1. Corporate benefits are a major part of compensation and should be taken as seriously as their pay.
2. As they start their first job, make sure your child understands important deadlines and the impact of their benefits choices.
3. Self-employed young adults can still find ways to create their own version of corporate benefits, especially health care and retirement plans.
4. Adapting to work culture will help your child succeed; make sure they are aware of their employer's expectations.

CHAPTER 11

Grownup Investing

Don't look for the needle in the haystack. Just buy the haystack!
— John Bogle

Ilove this quote from legendary investor John Bogle. Not only does it celebrate investment diversification, but it is also a great reminder that if we make investing too complicated, most likely our kids will just tune us out.

In the previous chapter we touched on some investing-related buckets like 401(k)s that might be available to your child when they start working. Now we are going to focus on what to do with that investment money and how to help your young adult child understand the different options that are available.

It is essential that we have a conversation with them about the difference between savings and investing, and make sure they are actually investing. What I mean by that is that we need to not just take their word for it that they are investing their money or that they will. We need to push to actually see what they are doing and make sure they are on track to accomplish the goals they have set. This may sound like I'm actually telling you to meddle in their business and do even more helicopter parenting, but stay with me here. There is a reason we need to really look at their accounts and see what is going on. You'd be surprised how many young people will put money into a brokerage account – or even a retirement account – without making sure the money is invested where they think it is.

When Ashley started her first corporate job, she proudly showed me how her 401(k) was all set up. I asked her where it was invested, and she replied, "In the 401(k)," with the expected *duh* facial expression. I then explained that she had to choose one of the mutual fund investment options offered in the plan. She asked me to pick one because she was rushing out and her friends were waiting. I insisted that she sit down with me, and together we went over what was right for her. She reluctantly sat with me for a few minutes, clearly losing patience and eager to leave. We decided on a diversified low-cost equity index fund to start. I tried to give her more information, but she kept insisting she would circle back later to learn more. I was frustrated but handed her the computer to actually choose the fund. When I went to look, she had chosen a fund by the provider of the equity index fund, but it was a government bond fund – not the one we had agreed on. She was already out the door. I decided that as frustrated as I was with her, it wasn't worth risking having her investments in the wrong place.

I made the correction for her while the screen page to her account was still open. A few days later I explained what I had done when we had time to sit down and go over it to make sure she understood and agreed. After all, it is her money. We've had a number of conversations since then, and I'm confident she 100 percent understands where her money is and why that error could have cost her a lot of upside in her investments. As the money has grown in the last few years, she is also more aware of how important those early contributions were.

Her younger brother, Bradley, was able to open a Roth IRA when he started earning money teaching fencing classes as a teenager. My husband and I made sure he understood the limits to how much after-tax money he could put in each year based on his income and how the Roth IRA worked overall in terms of rules and restrictions. We also let him know that once that was fully funded he could also keep saving and investing in nonretirement funds like a simple investment account at a brokerage, robo-advisor, or an investing app.

After he opened the account, he actively started looking for investments and asking questions. He came to me to suggest specific investments and questions, and we discussed different ideas. In the end, Bradley chose to invest in a low-cost ETF focused on the S&P 500, a very broad stock fund, and a diversified mix of technology stocks. He also chose to invest in one specific individual stock in which he had a personal interest.

While some parenting experts may disagree with how I handled each child's different levels of interest, there is no perfect solution. As our third child grows up, his needs and interests may be totally different as well. But what I hope you will agree with is that *I don't believe in standing on principle if there is an unintended long term financial cost.*

I also believe that we have to be realistic about where each of our kids are in terms of their interest in investing and in their financial independence from us. Sometimes they just aren't there yet – but will be very soon. They may need a push when it is easier for us to just do it for them or ignore the issue and hope things just resolve naturally one day. But as parents we are often doing a disservice to children by not pushing them to be adults. Sometimes the more passive they are, the more active we have to be at that time. They will be eternally grateful that we got them set up even if they didn't feel quite ready at the time. If we're being honest, were we even ready to be parents when we had them? I still don't feel ready to deal with kid issues a lot of the time.

Each of us as parents have to make our own decision about how much to step in and how much to let our kid stumble. When it comes to investing, do what is right for your family, but be mindful of the long-term consequences of letting a momentary slip-up impact their long-term financial success. It is a delicate balance, but we are stakeholders in our child's future, and we will pay the price eventually if we don't step up when we know, in our gut, they need the push.

When and Exactly How?

There are some life milestones that can at least serve as a roadmap to when your child should start investing their own money, but I want to stress that every child and family situation is different.

In theory it is never too early if your child shows interest and you have the resources to have them get started. Other good times to get them involved would be if they receive cash gifts for a birthday, holiday, or milestone, or when they start earning their own money.

New companies are emerging that make this easier. For my youngest, I use an app called Greenlight. We started using it for allowance but the company now offers an investing feature. Kids can research stocks and can invest with as little as $1, buying even fractions of stocks. My favorite feature is that the parent has to approve the trade before it goes through. It also has an investing feature with a platform to teach parents how to research stocks and other investments.

For the older children who were in their late teens when we got them started, my husband and I directed them to the discount brokerage firm where we already had accounts. This can be helpful because if the parents already have assets at a company, the next generation will often have access to more benefits and resources, because the accounts can be linked and have a higher total balance. They have access just like we do to a ton of research and educational materials to help them make decisions and learn about investing.

If your child earns money, or you give them allowance, they can use that money to get started. At holidays or birthdays when friends or relatives ask what to get your child, you can simply say that they are interested in investing and any contribution to his investment account would be welcome.

Brace Yourself

Your child may have very strong feelings about where to invest their money. They may, for example, be intrigued by all the discussions among their friends about Bitcoin and cryptocurrency. They may be hearing about trendy meme stocks on Reddit or TikTok. But this is where we have to be really careful about judging them and applying our investment rules.

Here is an example of why we need to listen and be open-minded to our kids' investment ideas and then let them take enough risk to either fail, ideally without long-term consequences, or reap the rewards of taking the risks they choose to take. In May 2020, during the beginning of the pandemic when everyone was home, the rental car business was hit hard. No one was going anywhere. Hertz declared bankruptcy. And then, while in Chapter 11 bankruptcy, the stock got a wave of social media buzz as young investors swooped in, buying the shares at ridiculously low prices. This made no sense. Professional money managers were baffled. When a company goes bankrupt, there is a long line of people who need to get paid, and the equity shareholders are way down the list. In most cases, they get wiped out.

Hertz was the one exception to that rule. Fast-forward to spring 2021, and as the country came out of lockdown and travel surged, demand for rental cars exploded. The company was sold at auction, and shareholders got a massive windfall. This was the perfect storm of events, but had you blocked your young adult from this investment you would have never heard the end of it. I was personally relieved my kids had not asked about it because I certainly would have told them to stay away – a mistake that could would have hurt our relationship.

In retrospect, the best course would have been to listen and then make sure they completely understood what was going on and allocated money only that they felt comfortable taking a huge risk with when they invested. The same approach might work for other investments that many of us might be skeptical about – and could be wrong about – like cryptocurrencies. We just don't know, so we should make sure to let them make their own choices. Our job is to ensure they understand what they are investing in and the risks associated with that investment. Let them fail – but also let them win.

Our young adults may have heard investing strategy buzzwords like diversification and dollar cost averaging and be curious to learn more. They may come to us with questions we don't know the answer to. It is essential that we welcome those discussions and not blow them off even if we don't know all the answers. It's fine not to know some things. I often go and look up exactly what something is because we are not walking encyclopedias. Let's say our child asks us whether they should invest in a mutual fund or an Exchange Traded Fund (ETF). We may have an idea about the difference but not remember the specifics of how each one works on the spot. It's fine to look up the information together and work through the right decision.

It is also completely possible that your child has done a ton of self-education, watched CNBC religiously for years, read the *Wall Street Journal* every day, and can teach you a thing or two. Be open to having a conversation about the investment choices you are making, and even consider asking for their perspective. You don't have to tell them the amount of money you have in each asset, but you could bond over a mutual interest in shares of Microsoft, Chipotle, or Alphabet. On the flip side, your child may be indifferent and just not care yet. They may say they will get to it later. They may say they can't afford to invest unless you give them the money to invest (don't give in!). They may be totally apathetic and tell you that you can just do it for them.

Wherever your child is right now, the key thing is for you to listen to them and understand their perspective, and then get them on track to accomplish their goals.

Ideally this conversation has been an ongoing one throughout their child-hood though casual conversations in daily life. If you started an invest-ment account with money they have received – for example, at birthdays from relatives and generous friends – this is a perfect opportunity to show them how money can grow over time. One way to get them interested is to look at the account together, the amounts you put in, how it has been invested, and how much it has grown over the years. A great time to start handing over control of at least some of these investments is when they get their first paycheck. Your child can get the satisfaction of putting money they earned working for someone else to work for them. Even if the account is set up so that you have direct visibility, let them know that you're available to discuss their investment choices but that they make their own decisions.

I benefited from this hands-on-but-only-to-a-point strategy with my Grandpa Bob. He generously gave me money to invest as a teen – but with some strings attached. Grandpa would gift me money every year and tell me that I could invest it in any stocks I wanted – but only if I came to him first and shared with him not only what I was going to buy but also explained the reasons.

Some years he would be very nonchalant and just let me figure it out on my own. But some years he would be very excited about a certain stock and really push me to look into it and consider that stock as my choice. He would explain why he felt it was a good investment and got really into whether it paid dividends and how he loved the fact that it provided income. It was a great discussion and a way to really get to know him. When I look back, I appreciate how wonderful it was to get specific guid-ance and to learn to take in and consider his advice. And I also liked that he was clear it was ultimately my choice.

Start with Goals

Your mission is not just to run through how to invest with your child. It is also to get them to care about investing and to understand why they are investing. One way to do this is to work with them on setting up short-, medium-, and long-term goals. From there, you can work with them on which kinds of investment accounts and what kinds of investments they want to choose to put into those accounts.

Short-Term Goals

This is money that will be used for the most immediate goals, which will depend on their age and what life stage they are in at the moment. Generally short-term is considered under two years. For a teen in their first job it might be saving up for a new tech gadget or trendy outfits – something discretionary you are not going to pay for. For an older kid it could be a car, and for a young adult it could be for a vacation with friends or an emergency fund. It should also include money to pay for their living expenses like rent and food. This is money that should be kept super safe and risk-free because they want to have access to it.

For financial educator and TikTok sensation Tori Dunlap, founder of Her First 100K, the emergency fund she had prioritized early in her career was a lifeline when she needed to quit a toxic job. "I had to quit after 10 weeks without another job lined up. But I had the financial stability to do that. I had an emergency fund where I was able to do that. At the time I spent three months unemployed."

For our daughter Ashley, her short-term goal when she got out of college was actually the final stretch of a long-term financial goal that started when she was a teenager. She wanted to save for a down payment on a first home. So, while living at home so she would have much lower expenses, she maxed out her retirement plans at her job and put almost all her after-tax earnings into super-safe accounts to build up the down payment in two years. I was proud watching her stick to that goal despite the incredible stock market returns her brother and her friends were seeing in their accounts. I had my doubts at times, because I saw the stock market rise while she methodically kept putting her paychecks into a savings account. But the market could have also gone down and taken her savings with it. She stayed focused on her goal, and about two years after college she had her down payment ready, along with money for closing costs.

Medium-Term Goals

This time frame is tougher to define and very open to interpretation. Medium-term goals often fall in the 2- to 10-year range but can vary depending on your child and their aspirations. The idea is to map out some things they think they might want to do in their next decade of life that will require money. Some examples could include paying for graduate school, buying a home, or having seed capital to start a business. I like to call them realistic dream goals.

Dunlap's goal was to have a net worth $100,000 by the time she was 25 years old – a goal she had not yet set when we first met. When she made the goal public, I was excited to watch and had no doubt it would happen. And it did. Dunlap stresses that her parents played a key role – including her dad's lessons on investing. "When I started making money, he was like, 'Let's talk about what a Roth IRA is.' And I was like, 'Okay, I've heard of it, but can you tell me more about it?'" They set up a time to talk, and her dad walked her through how to deposit money into an account and how to research stocks or index funds that she wanted to buy. Her dad took a very hands-on approach, having Dunlap watch him make investments and then in turn have her make her investments. "That was a collaborative process. He actually still has my login. Sometimes he'll log in and be like, 'Hey, your stocks are up today.' So, it was something that we sat down and did together, and he guided me through the process."

Long-Term Goals

This is in many ways the toughest one because it is so far off. Many young people are focused on just adjusting to all the grownup changes going on around them and feel a lot of financial pressure. Telling them to save and invest for a future that is more than 10 years out may cause some pushback. But addressing long-term goals, such as being financially solvent in old age and ideally being able to have financial stability and freedom, is mandatory. Investing early will make saving for retirement pain-free. A late start will be expensive and likely exhausting.

When I interviewed Ryan Serhant, from the reality TV show *Million Dollar Listing New York*, on my podcast, he told me about an app called FaceApp that will "age" you. He said that looking at the image of himself as an old man was scary – but also motivating. None of us really want to face our future as old people, but looking at that image will get a reaction – hopefully the one you want. Dunlap admits that even for her it can be really hard to convince 20-somethings to care about goals that seems so far away.

She likes to have her clients journal about future them. "Giving them context that you're not just saving for this arbitrary thing, that's decades away, you're literally saving for future you. Future me is 65 years old. She flirts with her Pilates instructor named Luca and she drinks Chardonnay with lunch in Palm Springs. That's the retirement plan." Dunlap has found that this exercise gives people a very detailed vision and a kind of manifestation of their older self.

Choosing the Right Buckets

Now let's get into where to put the money to accomplish the goals you and your kid have decided to focus on. We are going to cover the basics to get you started. There are entire books and endless options out there if you want to do a deeper dive.

Savings and Money Market Accounts

These kinds of accounts won't pay you much in interest, but they will keep your money safe. They are FDIC insured (up to $250,000 per account). Online-only accounts will often pay a better rate than more traditional institutions, so it can pay to shop around. This is where your child's emergency fund should be, so they can access the money with full confidence in a clutch situation.

Certificates of Deposit (CDs)

These can provide a little more upside for a medium-term goal but retain the FDIC insurance. They are not liquid so you can access the money only when the CD comes due, which will depend on the term you choose. The shorter the term, the lower the return. Shorter-term CDs can be a good option for money that can serve as an extra backup emergency fund with money that will become accessible in three to six months.

Bonds

Put simply, bonds are promises from companies or governments to pay a debt. Interest rates have been so low in recent years that bonds don't pay much in terms of their face value, and realistically your child probably does not need to directly own bonds. If they are interested in learning more they can research the differences between types of corporate bonds and various government bonds. The truth is that money is often made (or lost) in the trading of bonds, which is why it makes sense to buy them as part of a mutual fund. As we get older, bonds can often be a way to diversify and balance our portfolios, which again is often best done though a professionally managed vehicle like a mutual fund.

Stocks

This is where you will probably get your kid's attention. Stocks represent fractional units in a publicly traded company called shares. You know that expression don't put all your eggs in one basket? That's perfect for this. Unless your child is very focused and educated about the ins and outs of individual companies, has the time to keep track of their stocks, and has a very large amount of money to invest, individual stocks should probably not be the primary way they invest their money at this stage in their life.

That said, if buying a few shares of a company that interests them gets them excited about investing, that might be wonderful. Owning shares of a company that gets their attention – from Amazon to Disney to Microsoft – can be a fantastic conversation starter and a way to engage an apathetic teen or young adult.

Dividends

Be aware that there can be tax consequences to owning even one share of a stock and sometimes quite a bit of paperwork to manage. This can be another educational opportunity to engage your child about how stocks work and give them a choice that they can make after some learning. You can explain to them that some companies take a portion of their profits and distribute it to shareholders in the form of dividends. This usually happens once a quarter and on a per-share basis. Your child can choose to take the money right away or to buy more of the same stock with that money and have more shares. Buying more shares is often popular because investors can buy fractional shares, and it is a way of dollar cost averaging where money is invested automatically at intervals to smooth out stock fluctuations. Some companies offer dividend reinvestment plans (DRIPS), which also can offer discounted shares. Either way it is taxed as income.

Mutual Funds

This is a common option in a 401(k) and a popular choice for long-term goals. A mutual fund is simply a pool of money from many investors that is managed by a professional money manager. They can be a wonderful way to get diversification as well as professional money management at an affordable price. They can be for medium- or long-term goals depending on what is in the mutual fund. For example, a short-term bond fund can be a solid option for a medium-term investment, but for the most part, mutual funds will be best for long-term goals. The actual investments in the fund will vary but will generally include stocks, bonds, and other securities. It is important to look at not just what the mutual fund is called but also its actual holdings. Sometimes the title might not reflect what is actually in the fund.

It is also essential that your child understand the cost of the mutual fund. Fees for mutual funds can run the gamut. A fund that is passively managed and, for example, simply mimics a stock index should cost very little because a human is not selecting individual stocks. For actively managed funds, higher fees make sense because you are paying a human to actively decide what stocks to buy. Let your child do some research about how passive funds have performed compared with active funds before they make their decisions. There are also tax implications when investing in mutual funds, including dividends and capital gains. If your child (or you) feels overwhelmed, that's okay. Remember, it is not an all-or-nothing game. They can put some money in different mutual funds if that is their own decision. Our role is to make sure they make an informed decision.

Exchange Traded Funds (ETFs)

These accomplish many of the same goals as mutual funds, but often at a lower cost because of their structure. ETFs track investments like indexes, commodities, or other securities and can be traded on the exchanges just like stocks. Your child may have seen a commercial for the SPDC S&P 500. The ticker symbol is SPY. It tracks the S&P 500 index and is one of the most well-known ETFs. Unlike mutual funds, which can generally be bought and sold when the market is closed, an ETF provides the flexibility of being able to sell just like a stock at any time during the trading day. That makes it more liquid. It also has lower costs.

Non-Fungible Tokens, Cryptocurrencies, Art, Real Estate, and Other Investments

There are unlimited ways to invest money and endless information out there if you and your kids want to research more ideas. NFT's, Real estate, art, cryptocurrencies, and commodities are all ways to put money to work. They each have their own advantages and disadvantages, including cost, liquidity, and access to funds, and of course risk. For most young adults getting started, these should be a small percentage of their investments unless they are truly motivated to understand the risks and limitations and have enough funds to diversify appropriately.

Who's Holding the Money?

Where you put your money can matter a lot. Some places will offer what looks like a great deal. Free trades! But watch out, there are often hidden fees and customer service could be lacking. Some places will offer premium research and data that can be worth higher fees – if your child will be using it. Some will offer brokers that can meet in person, and some companies offer robo-advisors that can set up investing portfolios with little or no human interaction. And remember, while there are advantages to having higher total asset values at some places, your child can absolutely have money at more than one place.

Here are some options to consider.

Full-Service Brokerages and Money Managers

You may not think about it, but if you've been working, saving, and investing for a number of years, you may have quite a large account at whatever firm is managing your money. If that happens to be a full-service brokerage or money management firm, it may be worth looking into whether your child's assets will be counted as part of your extended family when it comes to assets the firm manages. That can possibly get your child a much lower commission rate or a higher level of service. It can also help them meet the minimum asset requirement many companies have. If the firm is smart, they will be very attentive to your young adult child to create an incentivize for them to stay and keep not just their assets with them but your assets down the road as well.

Odds are that even with a lower rate because of your family's combined assets, you are still paying a management fee. Make sure your child knows this and chooses to pay it. Go over the benefits and make sure that is something that your child will value. Many full-service money managers will try to add value through customized educational programs, extensive access to exclusive research, and other services to keep the next generation engaged. It is a personal choice if this is right for your family.

Discount Brokerages

These companies are going to be much more affordable but will not offer the premium services like personalized advice and guidance. Many will execute your child's trades for free – but choosing what to buy or sell and when to do it is a DIY strategy. While they won't get one-on-one investment advice, the larger discount brokerage firms do have a wealth of investment information so your child can self-educate. This is where our kids have their money right now, and it has been working well for them.

Robo-Advisors

These are automated portfolio managers that can have a lot of appeal to young people. Because they are less expensive than full-service money managers and brokers but don't require a DIY strategy, they can be a wonderful path to get started. They do charge fees, sometimes as a monthly percentage or as a fixed dollar amount, so make sure your child knows what they are paying. If they hold mutual funds or other investments that have their own fees, those should also be factored into the expense planning.

Robo-advisors invest money automatically based on information your child submits through questions about their assets, goals, risk tolerance, and more. As the market changes, and as your child gets older and their needs change, that information can be added to the mix and adjustments are made. It can have a lot of appeal for young adults who don't want to be hands-on but do want to reap the rewards of early investing with an affordable strategy.

Free Trading Apps

Robinhood led the way in this trend when it not only offered free trading but also created a gamification of investing. If this is something your child is interested in, it is important to listen to them and to stay close to what they are doing. These apps can tap into the same triggers that push people into addictive behaviors like gambling. Some people can use the app features responsibly, but many young people get themselves into a lot of trouble. There have even been cases of drastic behavior like suicide tied to the addictive behavior brought on by these kinds of apps.

One final note: Your own investment advisor, as wonderful and trusted as they may be, is not necessarily the best fit for your child. Dunlap urges parents to avoid what she likes to refer to as the "Steves" – her term for the parents' financial advisor who you've known and trusted for 10 or 15 years and – she warns this is a blanket statement – who is not going to understand what your 20-something child has in terms of life priorities. "They're also probably not going to be able to talk to your kid in a way that's actually going to get them excited about money."

Here is what one of her clients told her about her "Steve" experience: "My dad set me up with his financial advisor, but his financial advisor talks down to me or doesn't understand that I also have student loans to deal with or just doesn't explain things to me. He never explained to me what a stock was, and I'm confused." This kind of experience could set your child up for just not investing at all, despite all that you have done to get them excited about the process.

Review

1. Get your kid started investing now, if you have not already.
2. Make sure they understand the difference between putting money into an account and actually having it invested.
3. Show them by example how you invest, and then watch them make their first (and maybe ongoing) investments.
4. It's okay, with their consent, to have a login or access to seeing their account to monitor it and keep an open dialogue.
5. Give them access to resources to make their own investment decisions, but have them discuss their reasons with you.
6. Make sure they understand the risks associated with different investments, but don't be judgmental.

CHAPTER 12

Grownup Home Economics

. . . Ya wanna know what's great? Last night I woke up in the middle of the night to make myself a peanut butter and jelly sandwich . . . and ya know, it was my kitchen, it was my refrigerator, it was my apartment . . . and it was the BEST peanut butter and jelly sandwich that I have had in my entire life.
—Mare Winningham as Wendy in *St. Elmo's Fire*

No matter how basic our child's first home is, there will be something awesome about finally reaching that adulting moment of having their own place. But do they know what it will cost to live their grownup life?

One of the biggest budget killers for young people is just not knowing how much it costs day to day to run a home. Even if they attend college, they may graduate not knowing the basics such as how much food costs, all of the ancillary costs of running a home like utilities and repairs in addition to rent or mortgage payments, and how much just living life as a young adult can cost from socializing to buying their own clothing, tech devices, and even toiletries like shampoo and soap. And don't forget the toilet paper! Think how many things we buy for our homes that our children just took for granted would be there when they got home from school.

Everyday money life skills used to be taught in school but that is much less common now. Even if as parents we try to teach our kids financial lessons, our efforts might vary depending on what else is going on. In a perfect world, as our kids grew up, we would have taken them along with us, in person or virtually, as we shopped for our everyday needs, teaching them about pricing and how to get the best deals. In the real world we probably didn't bother, or did it rarely because it is easier to just get it done. And if I'm being candid myself, I often don't meticulously check the price of each item as I buy it so I would be a terrible teacher. But that is also because I am at a stage in life where just getting it done can override the time involved in doing a deep dive into getting the absolute best price on each item.

But if we haven't taught them at least to be aware of prices and make deliberate time-value decisions, now is the time to start.

I remember my sister telling me how early in her career, while working in marketing at a large consumer foods company, she and her colleagues were given the typical budget of one of their customers as part of their training. The task: go to the grocery store and buy enough food to feed a family of four on that budget, and see if they can afford to buy from her employer. She had to really look at each item carefully to get the right mix in order to complete the challenge. She was surprised to see how expensive their flagship cookie product was for the average consumer. If you can get your young adult to do this kind of thing – maybe as a competition – it might be a good exercise for both of you!

Jean Chatzky can relate to feeling like you've allowed your kids to be a bit out of touch from the affordability of their lifestyle. "If you've been providing a cushy or very comfortable lifestyle for your kids, they need an understanding of what they will and what they won't be able to afford on their own, whether or not you're going to be able to help them." Chatzky gives the example of whether they will take Uber rather than taking public transportation or walking. Will they be able to have a car and pay the insurance? What will it mean in terms of having money that will be left for groceries and whether they will be able to make their student loan payments when they move out of the house?

This has been a struggle in my family. We have tried and failed to enforce a budget on our middle child while he was in school because, based on the limited food and drugstore shopping options available in downtown New York City, we weren't sure he could do much better on price without taking too much time away from his various jobs, his fencing team practice, and his studies. We talk to him about the high prices, but we've become resigned to the fact that we have limited options in an extremely high-priced city – for now. He is spending responsibly and tracking where the money goes; it just doesn't go that far in the environment we've put him in (see earlier chapter on Lifestyle Inflation).

That's not to say we don't constantly work to get the best prices and then share our experiences with our kids. For example, I recently had to fill a prescription for our youngest child. The retail cost was over $900, the insurance copay was $200, and by using a manufacturer coupon I was able to pay $60. Knowing how to find the best price on things you need is a huge financial grownup lesson we all can use. I made sure that each child understood that the price you are first presented with is not always what you will end up paying, especially when it comes to things like prescriptions.

The Cost of Adulting

Whether your young adult rents or buys when they move out, it's important to understand how to protect their property.

Renting

When your child rents, they will likely have to fill out a series of forms that will include a credit check and references. Odds are you will also have to be on their first lease, so yours will be checked as well. They will also likely have to pay a deposit. Make sure they understand what that will be, and other costs just to get set up including landlord fees, and if they will have to pay movers. There may also be set up fees for things like internet access.

Next, it is important that they understand how the rent is paid – including whether autopay is available or required, when the rent is due, and what their rent includes. In some buildings it may include the utilities and even the internet fees. In some, those will be additional.

Renter's insurance will protect your child's belongings and could even provide an alternative place to stay if something bad happens like a fire, theft, or flooding. The landlord is responsible pay for insurance to cover the structure of the building. My personal experience helping Bradley get his renter's insurance was eye-opening. I first went to the traditional insurance company where I have had my homeowners' insurance for several decades. They acted entitled to the business and gave me a nonflexible – and in my mind very high – quote. The representative refused to give me detailed information on the phone about what it did and didn't cover. They informed me only that when I got the documentation for the policy I could read it but that it was all standard.

Fortunately, there are many alternatives now: companies with easy-to-understand language geared specifically toward young people. We chose to use Lemonade. I sat with Bradley and helped him work through the basics. He was able to put his information in and get an initial quote. But after that is where it got very impressive.

The system broke it down into different coverage areas that he could adjust to raise or lower the price he paid and what the policy would pay. For example, the initial basic quote offered him money to pay for a place to live if something happened to his rental. Since we live nearby, we knew he would just come home, so he removed that and his premium came down. The website also clearly explained each part of the policy and how it impacted the price he would pay.

Pro tip: Make sure when your child insures property, they are aware whether it is for replacement cost or actual cash value. Replacement cost will do just that: cover what it costs to get a new version of the item. Actual cash value will account for what that item was actually worth, which could be significantly lower than what it would cost to replace it.

Owning a Home

This can be more complicated because your child will pay real estate taxes and likely a mortgage. If this is the case, when they take out the mortgage, in almost every case they will be asked if they want to have the mortgage servicer also put aside money each month for the real estate tax. This is a great way to consolidate bills and make sure your child does not get an unexpected real estate bill at tax time. Remind them that part of the real estate tax as well as their mortgage interest will be tax-deductible. Also, unlike renting, utilities like electricity, water, and internet service are not included with a mortgage, so those should be budgeted for.

Homeowners' insurance is critical to protect their investment. Following our experience with Bradley, when it came time for Ashley's insurance we sent her to Lemonade. She had to have it in place in time for her closing, which was a cooperative apartment in New York City, so it was an important part of the homebuying process. She got started on her own, circled back to me and my husband for our take on how much coverage she needed and anything else she needed to know, and was able to get it all done on her own.

Could we have just done it for her? Sure. Could we have told her to just do what she thought was best and not give her advice? Sure. But this was the best balance of the two: she was totally capable of doing it herself but was also able to benefit from our experience as homeowners and was receptive to our guidance.

Creating a (Paper) Trail

Our kids will benefit exponentially for years if we help them get set up with a system to organize their money-related paperwork. It may be physical bills coming via snail mail, but more likely it's digital. This is where it is most important that we support our kids in how they want to set up a system because that will up the odds that they stick to it. But we should not assume they will do this without a little nudge.

The truth is, so many of us as parents have spent years muddling through with respect to our recordkeeping. Thanks to technology, so much work can be done for us. If you are still putting your various bills in something like a big folder or shoebox, this might be a motivator to move to a more intentional, and likely, digital system. Software like Mint, Personal Capital, and You Need a Budget (YNAB) is very popular. You have to put in the time to set them up and connect your accounts – and some do charge subscription fees – but they will give your child a clear picture of where their money is going and will help them map out where they actually want their money to go. Another great tool is simply using the sorting functions on their bank accounts or credit card websites to separate their spending into different categories and get a clear picture of their financial resource allocation.

Paper documents can create a mess. I still keep them because of my own personal comfort level, but for our digital native kids it might make sense to have them start out with a digital system. I have started using a scanning app whenever important documents come in and then uploading them to my locked and backed-up Dropbox folders. Make sure your young adults know which documents to keep. I also have a safe deposit box for essential paper documents where the original or a notarized version of the document is sometimes called for. That's a personal decision for your child, but they should have these documents in a safe place – and someone else should know where they are in case of an emergency. These would include official documents like power of attorney, their health proxy, passport, and birth certificate.

Home Maintenance

If your child is renting, the good news is that many things will be the responsibility of the landlord. Even in this case, make sure they understand exactly how to reach the owner or their representative, and the responsibilities that should be taken care of by the landlord. Depending on where they live, these landlord responsibilities may be part of the state's regulations. Make sure they understand the proper channels for reporting an issue and the realistic timeline for it to be fixed.

During a major storm earlier this year, my stepson's apartment building had a skylight break and water came rushing through his building's stairwell. While I wasn't thrilled to see the video he and his roommates took, the management company of his building was extremely responsive and had it fixed very quickly before too much damage was done. Knowing who to call when something bad is happening or something breaks is essential.

This might also be a good time to remind your young adults that you will not be arriving to clean their home. If this is not relevant to you, and your young adult is ready and willing to clean up after themselves in their new home, you are my hero and can skip this next part.

But for many of us, those years of picking up their laundry may not have set them up for success in that department. Make sure they know the basics of cleaning. At this point, everything from how to clean an oven to which products to use where is available in a YouTube video for them.

And if they want to hire someone to do it, that's ultimately their decision even if you don't approve. They just have to make sure they can pay for it.

Most of all: resist the urge to go over there and tidy up. Let go of them, and if it applies, let go of their mess!

Pet Projects

The pandemic puppy boom was real and was driven by young adults. According to Morgan Stanley's 2021 U.S. Pets Investing Trends report, 65 percent of 18- to 34-year-olds plan to acquire or add a pet in the next five years.[1] It's up to us to make sure they know what they are getting into financially. The report also found that 37 percent of respondents would take on debt to pay for a pet's medical expenses and 29 percent would put a pet's needs before their own. The cost of owning a pet doesn't end with the adoption or purchase price of the pet.

Medical Care

Just like every member of the family, pets will need regular medical care. This includes various shots, especially when they are young, and regular visits to the vet. A puppy often has to visit the vet every few weeks until they are 16 weeks old. Visits will still continue about every six months through life, and just like us, when tests are done, they are sent to a lab, so add those lab fees onto the budget. They will also need dental cleanings and various vitamins and medications.

Ongoing Expenses

Setting up life for a new pet will be expensive just as it is when a new human arrives on the scene. Depending on the owner's budget and priorities, costs might include:

- Food and treats
- Pet bed and toys
- Obedience training
- Pet-sitting and boarding

Insurance

One emergency vet bill can sink an entire budget, so if there is any way your child can afford to have pet insurance, they absolutely should. Plans come in all shapes and sizes, so they can be tailored to fit just about any budget. Typically, pet plans cover a percentage of the total bill after a deductible has been met; they often have waiting periods, so it's important to sign up before your pet needs it. If your child chooses not to sign their fur baby up for coverage, help them understand that they should set money aside every month so when something happens they'll have the resources to pay out of pocket.

Living Their Best Life

What does your child's life cost? It will probably make sense for them to put themselves on a budget, but even before that a candid discussion with you about how they want to allocate their everyday financial resources is probably a good idea. Have the conversation: Realistically where will they be eating? If so, can they afford that – and if not, are they willing to find new sources of income to support those choices?

The same goes for their going out budget. How often will they go out, and what will it generally cost? What will it cost to commute to their job? How do their financial resources compare with their peers? How will they navigate being pulled to an expensive restaurant for a friend's birthday or celebration?

While it may be tempting to lecture and really encourage our children to put up strict spending guardrails, ultimately it has to come from them. Some of our kids will be really motivated to keep their finances in order. Some will just go with the flow and figure it out along the way. Some will create a total mess and look to us to clean it up.

Regardless, we have to let our children decide how they want to start their adult life. Listening is everything, and if we try to control them and their spending we will likely be frozen out and watch helplessly as they sink or swim. We know we won't let them drown, but we have to wait until they at least call to ask for help and then make the judgment call.

Review

1. Setting up a first home is a huge financial milestone, and we should be proactive in helping kids create a protective foundation.
2. Insurance is a must whether our kids are owners or renters.
3. Budgeting and understanding spending should be discussed and systems put in place.
4. A document retention system will serve them well as their home finances – and general life documentation – start to grow.
5. Pets are great; make sure your kids budget for new members of their family.
6. Ultimately, we have to watch and wait and let them have their adulting moments.

Electives

CHAPTER **13**

Generosity

We make a living by what we get. But we make a life by what we give.
—Winston Churchill

A s important as it is for us to teach our children to earn a living, manage their money, and take charge of their life as financial grownups, we should not leave out lessons to be generous and supportive of causes in which they believe.

For Catherine Newman, this was a priority as her children were growing up. But it was also something that she felt should be presented as a regular part of money management. "I feel like they watch us make decisions about money, how much to give away in particular. We were always doing our charitable donations very much in front of them, just so they see the habit of it." Jean Chatzky says if you want to raise young adults who are givers, you need to lead by example: "You model giving and you include your children in your discussions about how much you give and why you give it and where you give it and you let them help make decisions about where some of that money goes."

One gift I was given by my parents was what I would call a charity allowance. They set up a Donor Advised Fund, which is basically a charitable investment fund with an immediate tax deduction. The assets can be invested and grow, and you can recommend donations to IRS-approved charities. As my siblings and I got old enough, our parents gave us an annual amount that we could give from the fund to causes we wanted to support. We still do it, and we all have access to seeing how much each member of the family – including our parents – gives to different causes and how the funds that remain in the account have grown.

I can't stress enough what a positive impact this has had on our family and our discussions around charitable giving and the importance of generosity. By setting up this system, our parents gave us the freedom to make our own decisions but were also able to see our choices and discuss them with us. My dad didn't tell us what to support but would definitely share his opinions. For example, he might point out that on a relative basis a fixed-dollar donation to a small charity could really magnify what they would be able to accomplish. That same dollar amount to a very large charity, while nice, might not have as much of an impact. As with any spending decision, we were asked to think: How far would our dollars really go?

Helping Your Child Find Their Causes

An infinite number of deserving charities need our support, but your child will likely have a finite amount of money to give. For that reason, help them plan how they want to allocate their resources. For example, sometimes supporting a small charity can have a bigger and more direct impact.

Make sure they look up the charity to verify its legitimacy and to understand what portion of the money donated actually makes its way to the cause. Keep in mind that the people who work as paid staff for a charity do deserve to be paid appropriately. Your child should make sure that a high portion of their donation is actually used for the cause, not just for administrative expenses.

One good resource for this is Charity Navigator, which rates charities based on factors like financial health and how transparent they are with where their money goes. The service is free and can help your young adult make sure the charity is legit and get a clear picture of how much of an impact the organization is making.

Religious Gifts

Many religions encourage their communities to donate money. For example, churchgoers are expected to tithe. Put simply that means donating 10 percent of your income to the church. In other religions, there are usually other giving expectations, often tied to significant things like a holiday, a loved one's memory, or an important celebration. Your child must make their own decisions, but letting your child know what you give and why can help them determine what is right for them. Also, many religious organizations are required make their budgets available to the public so you can see how the money is spent.

Corporate Matching Donation Programs

Some companies have extremely generous programs that will fully match your child's donation to the charity. If your child works for a company with one of these programs, encourage them to get to know the criteria first. For example, a common requirement is that the charity be a 501(c)(3) organization. Some companies limit the kinds of donations that they will match. An example may be that they match gifts only to colleges. This information should be easily available in the benefits section of your child's corporate website.

When Their Friends Ask

Odds are your child may have friends who approach them asking for financial support for charities. I've been on both ends of this. It may come as a simple ask for a fundraising campaign or in the form of an invitation to a fundraising event. Consider suggesting to them that they set up a yearly generosity budget for supporting causes that are important to their friends.

At a certain point, if the funds are gone for the year, they can simply tell their friends that they have used up their donation budget for this calendar year, but they will make a note to put them at the top of the list for the next year – and then actually do that.

Encourage them to always reply when asked for a donation, even if they can't give direct financial support, so the friend knows that they care. It's also worth asking the friend if there is another way they can support the organization. For example, if they are running in a race to raise money, could they come to the race that day and support their friend as a volunteer? Remember, they might be the next ones on the asking side.

Don't Forget the Tax Deduction

The tax law is always changing on this, but if your child itemizes deductions they should include charitable donations. Keep in mind that if they attend a benefit, only part of the ticket is likely a qualified deduction.

Review

1. Include a discussion about charitable donations in your money talks with your child.
2. Help them learn about how your religion views gifting and community needs and expectations.
3. Encourage your child to verify charities before giving using sites like Charity Navigator.
4. Prepare them to respond appropriately to friends' requests for charitable donations.
5. Corporate matching programs can stretch donations, giving them more impact.
6. Make sure they track their donations and deduct them from their taxes if they qualify.

CHAPTER 14

Driver's Ed

The car was the iPhone of the 20th century. Kids these days don't have to drive anymore. They just go there virtually.

—Jay Leno

Cars used to represent a teenager's first real sense of freedom and adult responsibility. Now that freedom generally comes first in the form of devices that allow them to connect without needing us, their parents, as conduits. That changed the role that a driver's license played, but it doesn't negate the importance of making sure your kids are ready for the responsibility of a car when the time comes.

When our kids were little, many of us spent countless hours in our vehicles transporting our kids to everything from school to activities and playdates. We made peace with driving SUVs and minivans and other adjustments we had to make as parents. Those of us in urban settings shuttled our kids around on public transportation and in taxis and Ubers and got used to coordinating logistics for our kids' often overscheduled lives.

Regardless of how our kids were getting to all the places, many of us looked forward to the day we could finally not have to plan our schedules around their schedules because we had to get them somewhere at a given time – and then pick them up from that place at a given time. And if we are being honest, many of us dreamed of the day we could finally get that cute little sports car guilt-free because we were done hauling around our kids, their friends, and myriad sports equipment.

For many families, especially those living in urban areas, the whole first car thing is simply not the life-changing milestone it used to be. My young adult children, currently in their early twenties, don't even have driver's licenses and have zero interest in driving. They walk or take public transportation almost all the time and occasionally take a taxi, Uber, or Lyft. If they want to go somewhere outside the city, they are comfortable getting on a train or finding a friend to drive them. As a parent, I do want them to learn to drive and have brought it up countless times. But it's their life, and I have come to accept that until they decide otherwise, this is how it will be.

But for parents whose kids need to be transported by car, how to handle getting kids into their own cars can be a tricky one because it is not just about their freedom – it is about our freedom, too.

In many ways having a car remains a key milestone of individual financial responsibility for a child as young as 16. How you as a parent structure their access to a car can set the stage for how other big milestones like home ownership will go.

Cars are expensive. If your kids buy it on their own, they'll either take out a loan that you will likely have to cosign, or drain their savings or investment accounts. Many parents choose to subsidize the cost of a car so their kids can get a safer or nicer one. Many parents allow their kids to use their cars or buy another family car that is designated for the child, and sometimes their siblings, to use and share.

Who Pays for What?

Buying a child a car on their big birthday is a popular image we see in the movies and on television, but it should not be a given. I say this as someone who did get a car when I got my driver's license, which was at age 17 in New Jersey where I grew up. I was the oldest child, and I knew it would be a shared car when my sister got her license. I remember shopping with my dad and him picking out a very moderately priced but high safety–rated car. I think I got to choose the color. Honestly, I've never been a car person and really didn't have strong feelings or a desire for a fancy car.

But the fact is, it was for my use, and I did not pay for it at all. I also did not pay for insurance, which I believe was wrapped into the family's plan to get a better rate. I paid for the gas using money I earned at my job at a local department store because it was hard for me to ask my dad for money directly since he was always very generous with his children. He never turned down a request for car-related expenses. I don't really remember any direct money discussions about getting a car.

In retrospect, I probably should have had more skin in the game. The truth is, on a practical level it probably was more important to my parents that they not have to drive me to things like that department store job, which was one town over and took 20 minutes to get to each way. I could also drive my younger brother and sister around. The car was for their convenience as much as mine.

Ultimately, each family has to do what is best for them as a family unit. If you can comfortably afford it, have a responsible child who understands the costs involved, and want to buy them a first car as a gift, that's great. Make sure they understand that this is not something they are entitled to but that you are gifting them and that you are also not committing to buying their cars forever. If you cannot or don't want to buy them the car, do not feel guilty. There are many ways you can support their goal of buying a car without spending your money – including helping them make the best decisions in terms of buying new or used, or leasing. You should also make sure they understand all the financial responsibilities that come with having a car.

Getting Ready for the Transaction

Before you actually shop for a car with your child, do some prep work. We can now do so much research and shopping online even if we do eventually want to actually do a test drive and make the purchase in person. Discuss the priorities with your child, get preapproved for a loan – which you may have to cosign – and come to an understanding of who will be responsible for the various financial costs.

The decision to buy or lease is both a financial and psychological question. I have always been a fan of owning a car I can pay off and keep for a long time. But I respect that many people have their reasons for leasing cars instead. The math can work for either one, depending on your personal circumstances and priorities.

The Case for Owning

While a car will depreciate over time, purchasing a new or preowned one is simple. If you buy it outright, you own an asset, so it's important to consider fuel efficiency and type as well as safety features. If you need to borrow money to buy the car, you make monthly payments until the car is paid off, but then you own it free and clear. The rates on these loans, which can come from the dealer or from a bank, credit union, or other lending institution, are often set very low to incentivize buyers. As is always the case, the better your child's credit score, the better deal they can get. Once the car is paid off, they will have no car payments, which can really create a sense of freedom – and also satisfaction of having accomplished the goal of paying off a sometimes substantial loan.

The number of years a car loan is spread out over, is getting longer because dealers want their customers, in this case your child, to see the lowest monthly payment possible. Be careful not to let your child fall into the trap of always having payments – even possibly owing more on the car than it is worth, because in almost every case cars go down in value as they age. As longer leases have become more popular, a trend has emerged of owners turning in cars to get new ones and taking out a loan to pay not just for what they owe on the new car but also the one they turned in. That is a disaster.

One of the joys of owning something like a car is the feeling of freedom when you no longer have a loan. If they need to spread the loan out more than about five years, your child should consider a more affordable vehicle, negotiate a lower price, or consider a preowned vehicle or leasing their first car even though it can cost more over time.

The Case for Leasing

Leasing a car has become very popular because your child can drive a more expensive new car than if they were to buy and have lower monthly payments. The downside is that the payments continue the entire lease, which is generally two to three years. If they lease one car after another, they will literally always have a car payment every month. At the end of the set time, they return the car and do not have an asset. There are often limits to how many miles they can drive, and if they go over it there will be penalties when they turn in the car. If they don't use the miles they have effectively paid for, they don't get any money back. There can also be wear and tear charges when it's turned in – so you want to make sure your child can keep that car in tiptop condition.

If your child chooses to lease, they will be driving a new vehicle, which will be covered by the warranty. Owners who drive their cars for a decade or more will have to manage repairs. New cars also will have the latest safety and comfort features. Other perks like free oil changes and scheduled maintenance are also often included, which just makes life easier.

Car Power

If your child has a source of income, this is an easy thing to have them pay for and feel a sense of independence and self-sufficiency. It will also help them understand the costs of adult responsibilities and experience one of the things that makes being a financial grownup so challenging. So much of what impacts our budgets and spending is simply out of our hands. As I write this in 2021, the costs of both cars and gas are rising aggressively. Every time we fill up our gas tank, the number is higher. We can't control this, yet it impacts all our finances.

If your child's first car is electric, congrats! While there are certainly other costs they will have to face, they will get a pass on the ever-fluctuating fossil fuel prices.

Insurance

While your child is still a dependent, this may be absorbed into the family ecosystem. Many insurance companies will add your child to a policy at a lower rate than it would cost to have them secure their own insurance. If this saves the family money, I recommend choosing that path for as long as possible, even if you decide to ask your child to pay the additional cost to add them to the policy. That said, make sure they understand how car insurance works as a condition of having them on your policy so they will be ready when the time comes to buy it directly for themselves.

Almost every state will require liability insurance for drivers. If your child does not have the required coverage they can lose their license, face fines, or even go to jail. But you want to have this because it protects your child and your family from personal lawsuits tied to an accident. It may be upsetting to hear, but if you have an accident tied to an uninsured driver – even if it is totally their fault – your insurance will likely be the one to kick in and pay.

You will also want to make sure to have collision insurance, comprehensive insurance, and personal injury protection. Collision insurance is for damage caused by an accident. Comprehensive insurance is for damages not tied to accidents like something falling on your car or a big weather storm that damages your vehicle. Personal injury insurance, while the name is self-explanatory, is worth just making sure your child is aware of it in case it is ever needed.

Another consideration is insurance that will help pay when your car simply breaks down. My family has AAA, but there are other options out there as well. For a very low annual fee, these services will provide towing and rental car coverage while your car is being repaired. AAA also provides discounts at countless retailers as a nice perk.

Other Factors to Consider

Your child, or your family if you keep them on your policy, will pay monthly premiums. Just like health insurance, you can often lower your monthly premiums by increasing the deductible.

While many insurance companies will charge more for teen drivers because of their lack of experience, taking defensive driving courses and looking for other good behavior incentives, such as good student discounts, rewarded by the insurance companies can help lower the costs.

Even if you are paying the insurance premiums, you might want to tell your child they are going to be responsible for any damage to the vehicle. Having discussed how insurance works, they will have a good understanding of the potential financial hit – another incentive to be careful on the road.

Are You Ready to Let Them Be Drivers?

Parents need to be able to let their kids face the consequences if they do break the rules as drivers. That seems simple enough on paper, but when you get to real-life circumstances, things get can a bit muddled.

Certified public accountant and financial wellness coach Kelly Long meets parents all the time who bail out their grownup kids rather than letting them face the adult consequences – because those consequences can have such long-lasting effects and at times have a financial impact on the parents as well. She shared one story of a mother whose 22-year-old daughter had been granted a large financial gift. There were conditions attached, including that she had to maintain good credit. Clearly the generous relative that left her that money put in those parameters with the best intentions. She simply had to be financially responsible. Unfortunately, the daughter was not financially responsible and would often get speeding tickets or not keep her car insurance coverage current. To protect the child from losing the money, the mom was paying the speeding tickets, going to traffic court with her daughter, and covering other costs to keep her out of legal trouble so she could still qualify for the gift. The daughter continuously left too late for her job and justified the speeding as necessary to get to work on time. She did not seem to understand the impact it was having on her mother and her mother's finances. What a mess.

Long explained to her client that by constantly rescuing her daughter she was enabling her child to continue this bad behavior and setting her daughter up not just for more trouble in the future but also for never-ending dependence that would weigh on the mom. The stakes would soon be higher because her daughter wanted to buy a home. "I said, 'If your daughter is not able to financially handle the identity of a good driver, how is she going to have the identity of a good homeowner? You need to challenge her; how do you think a good homeowner would behave here?'"

Long told the mother she had to think about her own approach. She explained that the mom's instinct to threaten her daughter – "If you don't do this I'm not paying anymore" and cutting her off – would just result in her daughter living with her indefinitely because she would not have the financial means to live on her own. She might even blame the mom or resent her because her mother had the means to give her financial support but was withholding it as a means of control. That was not a solution; if anything, it would be more of a financial hit to the mom. Long made sure the mother had an incentive to get this right. "I challenged her to approach it less from a shame perspective and more from a motivational perspective. Drawing a boundary and saying to her daughter, 'I can't afford to bail you out of this anymore but also I want you to think more about how your life is going to change when you have responsibility for a home.'"

Long found that guilt plays a huge role in parent's urge to help kids. They don't want to see their child suffer. Sometimes parents are so busy working, and given societal expectations, they feel like they've let their kids down. She sees this especially in families where there was a divorce. By doing things like giving them a car outright when they can drive, they think they are making it up to them. "It establishes this pattern where the kids are suddenly in charge of your wallet."

One approach Long recommends is to look at your own budgets and choose a set amount each month that they would use to help their children. "So for example, let's say it is $200 a month. I have $200 a month allocated to help you out. And when the money is gone, it's gone." Long has said that setting this boundary with a dollar amount can be helpful – if the parents hold their ground.

Review

1. Cars are often the first milestone to financial adulthood.
2. They can act as a testing ground for how your teenager will handle financial responsibility, set expectations for how much financial support you will be giving to them, and lay the groundwork for bigger adulting milestones like living independently.
3. The stakes are uniquely high when your child drives a car, because the financial consequences can impact the entire family.
4. It is imperative that parents make sure their new drivers understand the various costs associated with driving and that they are clear about their expectations of when those costs will be the responsibility of their child.

CHAPTER 15

Cultural Studies

*Financial health is a privilege that should be afforded to everyone –
and it starts with being willing to have the conversation while also
recognizing our own background and bias.*

—Erin Lowry, personal finance expert and author
of the Broke Millennial series

One of my concerns in writing this book was that I would bring a very specific perspective and approach based on my background as well as my own personal family and economic situation. We all see things from our point of view even as we do our best to try to understand challenges faced by others. Let's face it, each of us is shaped by our own experiences, including social pressures and expectations. We experience life from one vantage point: our own. For example, as much as we may hear about economic trends and stats in the news, to a large extent we experience an economy of one: ourselves.

While I have made deliberate efforts to interview and include experts of various cultural backgrounds and economic perspectives, it simply cannot be comprehensive. No matter what I do, I expect it will disappoint some of you. But I do want to at least try to provide some perspective and insights into the ways that our culture and community expectations impact our approach to parenting and to financial behavior and decisions.

Certified public accountant Anne-Lyse Ngatta of Anne-Lyse Wealth is the author of *Dream of Legacy: Raising Strong and Financially Secure Black Kids* and the mother of three kids. I spoke to her extensively about the unique challenges facing the Black community and how they connect to cultural expectations around wealth. As a financial coach, she is the go-to person for her friends and family when it comes to personal finance and sees firsthand the challenges facing even the most financially savvy Black men and women and their children.

Right out of the gate she expressed concern about the importance and unique challenges Black parents face in their efforts to teach their children to earn, grow, and retain wealth. "The statistics say that 70% of generational wealth is lost by the second generation and 90% by the third," she told me. "So it looks like even though we might be building the wealth, we are not doing a very good job at actually having conversations with our kids and teaching them how to build their own wealth."

The odds are already tough when it comes to creating and maintaining generational wealth. Centuries of slavery took a massive financial toll on the ability of people in the Black community to earn and invest effectively – and this continues to negatively impact the community today. Ngatta sees unique additional challenges in the Black community. She points out that there are systemic issues going back many decades, including unequal spending on education and widespread discrimination in the lending process. Obstacles like redlining, which prevented otherwise qualified buyers from living in certain neighborhoods, stopped Black families from buying homes and damaged their ability to create economic stability and generational wealth transfer.

Shawn Rochester, author of *The Black Tax: The Cost of Being Black in America*, points out that after 400 years Black families still own only about 2 percent of the country's wealth. He sees the challenges of a consumption-driven society and the lack of candid and open discussions in Black families about the importance of creating generational wealth. His message to Black parents, grandparents, and other older family members is to think: "How do you leave an inheritance for future generations? How do you put yourself in a position over time where you can retire with dignity? And then how do you also put yourself in a position where you can invest in things that really speak to you?" Rochester points out that as older generations accumulate resources over time, they can use them to help young people who need resources, but he adds that teaching young adults to be stewards of their financial assets and resources must come first.

Ngatta also cites lack of financial education about everything from investing education and debt management to negotiation skills as having been detrimental to wealth building. "Most of us don't have anybody to talk to who can teach us about those things. So we end up in a lot more debt than we should, and we spend the most part of our life recovering from it instead of actually building wealth." That's why she's so adamant that parents take ownership of the need to educate themselves. "I'm trying to encourage parents to be proactive and have those conversations with their kids, but it starts with educating themselves. I think a lot of times it's just even understanding the opportunities that are out there."

Some of the obstacles come from the community itself. For example, she explains that often in the Black community, when someone has financial success, they tend to want validation – and will spend to get it: "A lot of times when we do get money or when some of us become 'rich,' we tend to buy things that we just couldn't afford. And we tend to spend more money than I would say that a White person would. And I think it has a lot to do with just being perceived as insignificant by society. And finally, you get noticed, and you just have this tendency to just show your wealth more. And I think that that's something that we need to address as parents."

Rochester sees this as a reaction to anti-Black bias. "The way to counteract that is to show people through possession of certain things that you are more than. So your job and your title can do that, but also your car and your clothes and your home. If you are driving a nice car, the presumption is you must be doing well, right? As opposed to, you might be outside of your budget, trying to project that you're doing well." Of course, Rochester adds, for many young people, staying within their budget means missing out on that positive feedback from society.

That need to be acknowledged and taken seriously by society as a Black person is something even best-selling author Julie Lythcott-Haims admits had her spending more money than she should have when she was younger. On my podcast, she shared that as a Black and biracial young woman growing up in an upper-middle-class family, she desperately wanted to be a good representative of what a Black woman should be. "I was trying to not be the 'stereotypical Black person.' The credit card was like an appendage that was proving my ability or my worthiness or my right to be in these White environments. I overspent as a result."

Lythcott-Haims remembers plunking down her gold American Express card at dinner with friends as a way of showing both the restaurant and her friends: I have money – even though she didn't necessarily have money in the bank to pay that bill. And those were the consequences she didn't quite understand, despite being educated. Now as a parent, she and her husband, who comes from an upper-middle-class Jewish background, put systems in place to try to ensure their children are better equipped to manage their money. "When they turned 16, we decided it was time to give them a chunk of money that would be theirs to invest, with guidance. We want them to understand that managing money is, yes, complicated, but that it's also interesting, important, and doable."

But for the broader community, Ngatta still sees a frustrating pattern: "I think we spend a lot more money on clothes, designer stuff. We spend a lot more money on fancy cars and more than I guess White people would do," she tells me. In her opinion, the spending is often a consequence of Black children growing up feeling like they don't matter, so when they do start to have money, they want to make a point to show that they matter and are worthy of the same attention as everyone else.

Ngatta stressed that all parents who may feel the need to use money and spending to get noticed – especially parents in Black communities – must teach children that their net worth has nothing to do with their self-worth. She warns that if parents don't teach kids to value themselves, they will grow up trying to compensate through money: spending it and buying things so they can feel validated. In her family, she does daily affirmations with her twin girls. The first thing they say is, "I'm a beautiful Black girl," because she feels the world will tell them that they're not. Lyse also sees financial misinformation prevalent in the Black community on some very basic concepts and is working to get the correct information out. "The concept that you should carry a balance on your credit card. It's good for your credit score. So even just sitting down with them and walking them through your process, that you pay off your credit card balance every month and explaining to them why it's important, walking them through the process of looking at their credit report, walking them through the process of investing in the stock market."

Ngatta is also frustrated by what she sees as extreme pressure on those who earn and invest money well to then support members of their extended family, making it harder to retain and grow wealth. Add to that the fact that because the older generations often do not have enough money in place to retire, their children often step in with support. "The expectation is not that you are going to just take care of your family and your kids. The expectation is that you are going to probably take care of tuition for other people's kids and that you will probably take care of your parents." One reason Ngatta has been able to be successful as a financial grownup is because she did not have this responsibility. Her parents were financially independent. But she is adamant that her case is, unfortunately, often the exception.

Economic differences, regardless of race, are also going to shape how parents communicate to their children about money and their financial responsibilities as they mature into adulthood. Lythcott-Haims agrees, pointing out that in many cases poorer families have greater financial discipline – because they need to. "Working poor and working-class families do not have the discretionary income to make those mistakes. Instead, they're teaching their kid, 'You need a job. You need to pitch in.' I think kids who grow up in such families are deeply aware of every dollar spent on their behalf." Lythcott-Haims encourages parents regardless of their economic status or race to make sure their young adult children have a hunger to not just earn money but to manage their own money and finances and to understand the benefits of delayed gratification.

In her case, Lythcott-Haims's son took a year off from college and had a minimum wage job at Safeway at the deli counter when he was 20 years old. He hadn't worked in high school because she and her husband had wanted him to focus on his academics, which is not unusual for parents in her upper-middle-class community. "Boy, did that kid learn a lot: how little you make, how much the government takes, how to budget for his food and his utilities and his rent and all of that. But he also learned the deep satisfaction. When a manager came over and said, 'A customer just came to us and complimented you,' it is far better than any accolade a parent can offer."

Rochester stresses the important of influencing the early career decisions of young adults, and making financial upside, potential savings, and investing the focus. "Choose careers where you can earn a lot at an early age, then save as much as possible. If you choose a low-earning career, then it's so much more difficult. The difference of careers could be $2 to $4 million of lifetime earnings."

For CFP® professional Pam Capalad, of Brunch and Budget, the concern is often clients who are not only people of color but also first-generation Americans. She cofounded the Race and Wealth Podcast network and runs a financial planning program called See Change specifically designed for people of color. She works with immigrant parents who don't know what they don't know and for cultural reasons do not want to talk to their kids about money. Their parents did not talk to them. "I've definitely had some parents who have straight up yelled at us and said, that is none of my kid's business."

She worries about immigrant parents from different backgrounds and economic systems not understanding the delicate balance between using debt and credit for positive things and being in debt. "I've seen parents tell kids, especially in families of color in particular: don't get into debt at all. Debt is bad. Don't get into debt, don't get a credit card. They don't explain why, and they don't explain what credit cards are, but they most likely have had a bad experience with a credit card."

In some cases that Capalad has seen, the parents have been paying off debt for several years, so they tell their kids not to get credit at all. "I've had clients, they're like 26, 27, and have never had a credit card. And all of a sudden they have to rent an apartment and don't have a credit score."

She also sees well-meaning clients who put paying for their college ahead of their own retirement savings. "A lot of our clients are people of color, first-generation college graduates. They're often taking care of their parents on the other side already. They're often the breadwinners for their extended family in a lot of ways. So, their thought in their head was, 'I have student loans and I don't want my kids to have student loans.'"

She has also seen the educational system leave kids with more debt than opportunity. "I think that we were taught for so long that like college is the way to go. And especially kids of color were like, 'Go to college. When you go to college, you'll come out, you'll get a good job. You'll make more money than your parents did. You'll have a professional salary, all of these things.' And we're seeing that, that hasn't been the case."

Capalad and her team push clients to understand that the biggest gift they can give their kids is knowing that they don't have to take care of their parents in retirement. "It's easier to prioritize your kids than it is to prioritize yourself because that's what your parents did for you." Capalad herself is an immigrant; she was born in the Philippines and remembers having to figure out a lot of money-related concepts herself because they were so foreign to her family. "My parents aren't from this country, and they didn't experience the way that the debt system works, and the tax system; they're not going to know to explain it to you. You're probably explaining it to them. And that's a lot of my clients' situations. They were the ones helping their parents do their tax returns."

Tori Dunlap sees this pattern in her clients as well. "I hear from a lot of women of color who are first-generation Americans and whose parents didn't counsel them at all, who are often also responsible for their parents' retirement." She adds that they are often also taking care of their parents' health insurance, and then as they become parents themselves have to focus on their own children's upbringing. "That is a huge burden that we're not talking about enough, especially with immigrant families, with families of color, there's this multigenerational responsibility."

Dunlap also stresses the need for gender equality in teaching our children about finance. "I have so many clients who had brothers, and their brothers learned how to invest. Their brothers learned how to negotiate their salary. But the daughters were left out of the conversation." She says they were often taught to budget or clip coupons. They were not taught wealth-building strategies or how to invest or advocate for themselves at work.

As parents, we need to make sure we give equal support and financial education to all of our children and not favor the men.

Review

1. Cultural differences in how we approach financial literacy are real and should be acknowledged.
2. If you as a parent are aware of cultural and community expectations or pressures that will impact your young adult, point them out and help them strategize on the best ways to navigate those challenges as they grow into adulthood.
3. Hands-on experience in jobs benefit kids of all backgrounds and can teach priceless lessons at all income levels and cultural communities.
4. Do a self-check and make sure you are educating young adults of all genders equally.

Exmissions

CHAPTER 16

Til Death Do Us Part

From the moment I first saw you
The second that you were born
I knew that you were the love of my life
Quite simply the love of my life

—Carly Simon

I share the preceding quote because the song is often mistaken for being about a romantic partner, but it is in fact about a parent's love for their child. For many parents, the strongest bond until the day we die is with our children. If you are reading this book, you care enough about your child's future that you will be tied to them as long as all of you shall live, and your financial choices will impact them well after you have passed. It's a natural biological instinct to want and need to take care of our offspring. It doesn't magically go away when they hit a certain birthday. Children really are the love of our life.

That is exactly why we absolutely need to take a deep breath and face the fact that it is in everyone's best interest to make sure kids have visibility into what happens when we pass. While we don't have to share all the details of where our money goes when we are gone, or a full accounting of our assets, we do have to make sure they know where to find that information and what their role will be. You may be clueless about this, so think about how they must feel – they don't know what they don't know. And speaking as both a parent and a child, I hate this topic.

The ick factor of this resembles the sick-to-your-stomach feeling that likely accompanied the first talk you and your partner had about money. You want to put your best foot forward. Who wants their kids to worry? We want them to always think we've got it all under control, so they feel secure. There may be things that aren't as solid as we wished they were, and we want to avoid sharing that with them. As much as we want to have open conversations with our offspring about their financial plans and goals, what happens after we pass will also have an impact on their financial futures. For some who are in a position to pass down an inheritance, we may not want them to know about it, because it could impact their motivation to succeed on their own. It also may make them feel as if they might not be able to live up to our financial success. It is a psychological minefield.

Another concern is that we don't want our kids to see our weaknesses and our financial failures. They may think we are sitting on a very comfortable retirement when in fact we are barely scraping by and putting on a brave face. The truth is many of us avoid sharing and just hope for the best. After all, we won't have to clean up the mess. We should think carefully about the consequences of keeping our kids in the dark, though. A mismanaged estate can do serious damage not only to their financial futures but also to your family's relationships.

And if that does not scare you, think through what would happen if they needed to take care of you unexpectedly for a long period of time. Do they even know where to begin? Could they pay your bills? What if you lost your home because they simply did not know how to make sure your mortgage was paid on time? Do they know where your financial documents are? Do you have a system for them to get into your electronic files? Do they know if you have long-term care insurance – or even what that is? At the most basic level, do you have a professional in place who your kids could go to and alert, who would then do all these things and more?

This is where the pandemic may have created an opportunity for a conversation. Whether our kids were living with us or not, we were most likely in touch more often during those months. My family, for example, had weekly Zoom chats with my dad and stepmom and my siblings. There has been a new kind of dialogue happening between grandparents, parents, and adult kids.

Catherine Newman experienced this in her own family. "It's like this weird pulling back the veil and the pandemic's great for this because a lot of people are home a lot now." Newman says having kids at home created a natural opening for conversations that the kids might not have been mature enough for when they were teenagers in the house before going to college. Adult children moving home to quarantine was an opportunity to live together as a family during a different life stage from the norm. When families were all living together before the pandemic, most were often too busy with activities, commuting, day-to-day errands, as well as work and school pressures. COVID-19 presented the opportunity for quiet, uninterrupted family time and the natural flow of conversations in a comfortable setting.

As a society, someday we will likely be able to look back and recognize the pandemic as the spark that led to more families talking openly about the parents' end-of-life needs and expectations. What would have happened if a parent was ill? Is there a health care directive? What about power of attorney? Do they know where all the financial records are kept? Do they, quite literally, know how to manage your daily finances if you were to get sick? What bills must be paid? Could they recognize a scam? If you have designated a professional to do that, do your kids know who that is to make sure they are in the loop and can step up? What questions do they have about your estate planning? What do you want to tell them about your financial wishes for after your pass?

This Is Awkward

Starting a conversation about death is uncomfortable. I know every time one of my parents brought up their money and what happens after they pass, I immediately panicked and assumed they were ill and not telling me. I tried to avoid those conversations. I did not want to be ready for them to not be there because that meant that one day they might not be there. I chose denial. That's always the wrong choice.

So it is important for us parents to reassure kids that nothing is prompting the conversation – everyone is fine. Of course, if something is wrong, it is essential that you be clear and not waffle in your communication. Our instinct as parents is to minimize the stressors in our lives when we're talking to our kids because we don't want to worry them.

Don't be put off by the term *estate planning,* which can sound like something only the super-wealthy need to do. In reality, estate planning is simply planning for what happens to our money and to the people we take care of when our lives end. It applies to everyone.

Vicki Cook, coauthor of *Estate Planning 101*, was working on her own parents' estate planning documents and used that as an opportunity to connect with her adult children about the topic. "They saw and heard the conversations that we were having with our parents about what their wills are, what their final wishes are. It's an emotional topic, but this is important. Like, we need to know this, like, how would I know what you'd want if we don't talk about it?" She framed the discussion like this: "When you're an adult and you have people to take care of, this is part of taking care of them." Cook also created her own estate-related documents at that time and made sure to talk to her children about them. She did not go on excessively about it. She had the conversation, answered their questions, and then moved on.

You Don't Have to Bare All

While you do have to make sure your kids know some things, that does not mean they have to know all the details of your estate planning. "We didn't get into all the money and, you know, who's getting what and all of that," says Cook. "It's just that we have a plan and here's where you can access it should anything bad ever happen to us. And that we hope it doesn't, at least for a long time."

Amy Blacklock, coauthor of *Estate Planning 101*, advises us to share what we are comfortable with based on where we are in our life, our relationship with our kids, and where they are in terms of their ability and interest in understanding the situation. "You need to give them enough information so that they know you do have particular assets, but they don't necessarily need to know how much that money is if you're not comfortable sharing that," she says. "And I think a lot of it might just depend on their age as they get older. Maybe you're going to be a little bit more willing to share things."

Blacklock also stressed that this is an evolving conversation that should be revisited periodically as circumstances change and create the need for adjustments in your family's plans. That may be at different adulting moments, like when a child gets married or has a child. It may be when you have a life change that could impact your plans.

No Lottery Winners

Make sure your kids are ready for an inheritance. A child who is not prepared to responsibly manage a financial windfall could spend their inheritance in a nanosecond.

Anne-Lyse Ngatta saw this firsthand with a friend who was used to a lavish lifestyle. When her father passed away and she inherited a substantial sum of money, the friend spent close to a million dollars in three years and did not buy one asset. "She bought a lot of designer clothes. She traveled all around the world and she didn't have a house. She didn't even have a car." Ngatta explains, "She grew up kind of like living very lavishly, but the parents didn't take the time to educate the kids on how to earn money, and that's just the lifestyle that she was used to. And she just continued on."

I have no doubt her friend's parents were generous and simply wanted their daughter to live a wonderful and financially comfortable life. But those good intentions backfired because she had no guardrails set up for her when she suddenly had access to all that money.

If you have any doubts about your children's ability to manage a sudden inheritance, get a trusted and qualified loved one or a professional involved, and consider setting up a trust to protect the assets immediately. The danger is real, and the repercussions are painful.

Extenuating Circumstances

Speaking of getting a professional involved, there are cases where no matter what you do, your young adult child is simply not ready or able to oversee their finances if something should happen to you and their other parents or guardians. That's when it's critical to have a system in place, says CPA and personal finance specialist Michael Eisenberg. He urges parents to be realistic when it comes to their young adult's ability to handle money if they are gone. Some will not be ready to take charge of their financial assets, and will need trusted and well-vetted professionals involved at different levels based on their needs, even if they are no longer legally minors. "Unfortunately, there are kids in that age bracket and then they get older that do have certain handicaps, if you will, whether it's addiction or mental issues or whatever it is," says Eisenberg. "And you need to be cognizant of that. Sometimes the parents don't want to talk about it."

Siblings can also play a meaningful role if this is the case, according to Eisenberg. "If you're not around, for example, which one of your children will be able to step into your, the parent's, shoes to help to take care of your brother or sister." This is something parents should discuss together with that sibling. Eisenberg also suggests putting spendthrift clauses into trusts so that the kids can't blow the money. A third-party trustee can often be a good choice over a close relative because the former is removed from the situation. It's better to avoid putting a relative in the position of having to say no to your adult child because that could put a strain on the relationship. They also may not have a complete understanding of the responsibilities and even unintentionally make some errors. A professional trustee can put up guardrails to make sure your wishes are carried out.

The Basics of Getting It Done

If you already have a plan, make sure it is up to date. Anytime there is a milestone in your life – or every five years, whichever comes first – review it to make sure changes aren't needed.

If you don't have a plan for what would happen if you were not around to take care of your kids, now is the time. The first step is to understand what documents are needed and why. It is generally best to involve an attorney, but a number of solid DIY options are emerging that we'll discuss later in this chapter. The stakes are high, and it is essential that you understand what you are signing.

Advance Directives

- **Health care proxy:** Make sure you have someone with the authority to make medical decisions if you become incapacitated. This is a very simple form that can often be done through your doctor.

- **Living will:** This can be general or very specific, but it essentially will create a roadmap for your care should you not be able to communicate it directly. For example, you can specify that you do not want to be kept on life support if you are in pain and the doctor determines that your condition is terminal.
- **Power of attorney:** This is someone who can act on your behalf to carry out financial decisions. For example, they can make sure that bills like your mortgage and various insurance bills are paid on time.

Insurance

- **Life:** For most people, term life insurance will be sufficient. It may make sense to consider staggering a few policies so that you have maximum coverage when the kids are younger and then as the need for support subsides, you have less. If you would like to have an investing component, whole life could be considered. Keep in mind that whole life often has a commission for the person who is selling the product.
- **Long-term care:** This is totally different from health insurance and in fact covers things that health insurance will not. For example, if someone has a chronic illness, disability, or ongoing disease like Alzheimer's, it can help pay for home care or assisted living with daily activities.

Wills and Trusts

- **Wills:** Everyone should have a will. It may sound intimidating, but a will is a document that shows where you want your assets to go after you die. People get really emotional about it and procrastinate making a will, but once you get it done you will feel so much better. I avoided it for years. That is ridiculous, and I regret it. If you do not have a will when you pass, the state laws will kick in and will decide who inherits your assets. Make a will because it is a final gift to those you love.
- **Trusts:** A trust provides more privacy than a will. Put simply, it's a legal arrangement made among three parties:
  - the trustor, or the creator of the trust
  - the trustee, or the person who oversees the trust
  - the beneficiary, or the person who will benefit from the trust

A trust will give you control over things the like timing of when the assets are distributed, can protect the assets, and in some cases can have tax benefits. It can go into effect as soon as you establish it, so it can be useful in both life and death. It might be helpful if you have minor children or a family structure or business that may be complicated. Examples include blended families, unmarried parents, special needs children, or a multigenerational family business. They can be much more expensive than a will, and they may not be necessary in the short term. While you should always have a will in place, a trust may not be needed.

WE'LL ALWAYS HAVE PROBATE   Probate is awesome – said no one ever. Even if you have a will, your estate will go through probate. If you die with a will, the court will need to validate the will to ensure that your representative distributes everything properly. If someone wants to dispute the will, that goes to the probate court.

If you don't have a will, your loved ones will have some headaches. Dying intestate, which means without a will, gives the power to the state. The probate judge chooses an administrator to manage your estate and decides who will be the guardian for your kids if they are still minors. Someone you do not know could end up raising your kids. The law will decide who gets what in terms of your assets. So if you always wanted a friend to get a special necklace, forget it.

AVOIDING PROBATE   Certain assets, if they are properly documented, can go directly to beneficiaries, so it is essential that you make sure everything is in order. That saves time and money and keeps things more private. This is also a great conversation to have with your young adult kids who are working in jobs with retirement benefits.

Some examples of assets that can bypass probate include life insurance policies, trusts, and some investment or retirement accounts. Bank and brokerage accounts that are designated as Payable on Death (POD) or Transferable on Death (TOD) can also avoid probate. To get them reregistered, the beneficiaries need to present a death certificate. Also of note: jointly owned assets are not subject to probate.

A Note about Technology and Passwords

Make sure someone can get access to your files not just if you pass away but also if you are in a position where you can't manage your finances, such as a health emergency. One way to do this is to use a password manager. Most have affordable family plans and have an emergency access feature that lets a loved one access your passwords if you are nonresponsive for a certain period of time. The person can also have access to your digital legacy, which likely includes a lifetime of photos, video, and other precious memories.

You simply go into your settings of your password manager and designate a trusted person to have emergency access. Most password managers will then walk you through the steps to finish the set-up, including setting up a waiting period, which is how long that person must wait before gaining access. That gives you time to deny their request if in fact there is not an emergency.

However, if you were, for example, in an accident and under medical care for a few weeks and you had given a loved one access to your passwords after a 72-hour waiting period, they could go in and make sure your bills were getting paid or put an appropriate auto-responder on your emails.

The Kids Need a Plan, Too

Blacklock says that while young adults often don't need to do everything right away, there are some basics parents should push them to get done as soon as possible – starting with the financial power of attorney and the medical directives. This is something they can and usually should do as young as 18.

Full disclosure: until I was writing this book, I had never really thought about it. The laws vary by state, but if as parents you want to be the ones in charge if something happens, life will be easier if you have this set up. "You could share with them how even when they go away to college, if they got real ill there, that without these documents, you might not be able to have a say in their medical care, their treatment, you might not be able to help pay a car payment if they have a car or pay the rent on their apartment. If they have a lease, you might not be able to do much if they don't have these power of attorney documents in place," says Blacklock.

While it's never a bad idea to have a will, if you are getting pushback Blacklock says that if your child does not have assets, they probably can wait on that if they are okay with their assets being subject to probate and state law. They should also make sure they have deliberately named beneficiaries for any investment accounts that they have, including their 401(k) and IRAs. This will help them avoid probate, which is costly and public. The same goes for making sure that they have named beneficiaries for life insurance and POD bank accounts.

Paying for It

No one wakes up one day and decides to splurge on estate planning. That's why if we want our kids to step up (and frankly this goes for us as well) it is essential that we also help them figure out how to pay for it. The good news is that there are a lot of good resources out there.

One option that kids may not even be aware of are the free or subsidized legal and insurance benefits that come with their jobs. For example, many employers offer some basic life insurance for free. Sometimes they even offer life insurance for a spouse. They also may offer disability and umbrella insurance.

One often overlooked benefit is legal services. These usually require employees to sign up at open enrollment and commit for an entire year but can be a great deal. The plans typically give access to a network of lawyers who will do basic legal tasks like wills and trusts for either no fee or a very low fee. Think of it like an HMO but for legal work.

Cook and Blacklock stress that while lawyers are usually the best choice, new resources like LegalZoom.com, RocketLawyer.com, and TrustandWill .com might appeal to our children. My own young adults ages 24 and 21 used TrustandWill.com to create basic wills and an advance directives and had a very good experience. There were prompts and easy-to-follow directions as well as resources if they had questions. I sat with the 21-year-old as he went through each screen, and we discussed his decisions as he completed the forms. If your young adults complete documents online with a service like this, they must follow up and get them notarized or they will not be valid.

Review

1. Bring your kids into the discussions about what will happen financially when you pass.
2. Parents do not have to reveal all of their plans, but they do need to make sure their children know where to get the information they need.
3. If there will be an inheritance, make sure the kids are ready or that you have guardrails in place to protect them.
4. Do not overlook the importance of having a way for your heirs to access digital accounts.
5. Your kids need to do their own will and advance directive if they are 18 years old or older.

CHAPTER 17

Stepping Back: A Parental Pep Talk

I realized if we wrote the check, it would just be putting off the inevitable.

—Liz Weston, CERTIFIED FINANCIAL PLANNER™ professional and author

At a certain point, we have to launch our kids into adulthood – and that includes being financial grownups. The age that each of us thinks of our children as adults is personal, but we need to come to grips with the fact that it must happen. If we keep giving them financial support, we need to understand why we don't trust our children to figure it out how to be their own financial grownups. As we've discussed, we can be generous with our kids, but we all know the difference between generosity and bailing them out of situations they should be able to handle themselves. In practice, this may put us at odds with our kids – hopefully only temporarily. We may be frustrated and feel they aren't listening to us because of course we know better and just want to protect them.

I was recently at a wedding, and a couple my parents' age asked what I was working on. When I told them about the book, they looked concerned. They said they worried about meddling and that telling their kids what to do with their money would alienate them. In fact, they told me that when they tried to talk to their kids about money, the kids simply did not listen. My question is this: Are we listening to them? Are we tuned in to what they really need or don't need from us? At a certain point, they *need* to not need our help and to reach out on their own when they *want* our advice and perspective. While the wait can be frustrating, if we have the strength to give them the right amount of space, this will likely happen. As much as there are strategies for getting your kids to launch, sometimes we will find ourselves at a loss. As they say, there is no magic bullet. And if they are financial grownups and totally self-supporting, it's okay to let it be and stand back while they make mistakes we see coming.

Leslie Tayne has done everything she can to proactively make sure her kids understand her expectations for them as young adults, yet even she has been in some incredibly frustrating situations, despite doing everything she could to set them up for success. When her kids were old enough to drive, she kept a second car for them to use and paid the insurance. She required them to have a job and pay for their own gas. She would overhear them griping about the cost to fill up the car and making choices about where they would go, knowing that cost. All good, right? Not so fast.

That didn't protect her from the fact that at the end of the day, teenagers sometimes have bad judgment. They are programmed to push for independence from their parents, but their view of independence comes through a very different lens at times. One night, Tayne got a call from her daughter saying that her son, who had only a learner's permit, took the car out in the middle of the night with a bunch of friends, which is of course against the law. She was furious. He could have not only injured or killed one of his friends or himself, but also put the entire family in financial and possibly legal jeopardy. "I said, you don't have a driver's license; you have no right to drive my car under any circumstances. If you would have had an accident or something would have happened you would have, single-handedly, ruined everything I built. I don't think you understand what that means, what the financial consequences of that are." She suspended his driver's permit and told him she was not going to allow him to get his driver's license.

Her son was defiant, claiming everyone drove their parents' car and that she was overreacting. He tried to make the argument that without a car she would have to drive him everywhere – which was actually a pretty smart tactic. One of the most common reasons parents get kids cars is so they can avoid being a chauffeur. But Tayne held her ground. "I had a cop come to my home and talk to my son about what the consequences would have been, because he still kept saying to me, 'You're making such a big deal.'" She never got him his own car, and the kids had to share the one car. She said she could have afforded another car and it would have been easier on all of them, but she wasn't going to do it.

Eventually, Tayne had a candid conversation with her children, explaining that while she would be there for them she would be setting limits from that point on. "It is now time for me. I have spent all of my money for my entire adult life on you guys. And I love you. And I cared for you, and I've provided this yellow brick road for you, but I'm done. And from this point on the money I make has to go into my retirement and my future because I need to be able to take care of myself." Part of her motivation was that as much as she loves her children, and as much as she believes they would want to take care of her, she says she would not rely on them to take care of her.

That doesn't mean any of this is easy. "The really tough thing is watching your kid fail, if you could step in and fix things," author and CFP® Liz Weston tells me. Weston remembers a time when a young family member was in an awful financial bind and she and her husband could have written a check to get her out of it. "But she was making bad decisions, and the bad decisions were compiling on bad decisions. And I realized if we wrote the check, it would just be putting off the inevitable." Weston says it was hard not to step in – and it's even harder when it is your children. If they are showing a pattern of bad decisions and poor judgment, at some point we have to let them suffer the repercussions. Says Weston, "If you keep bailing them out, what's the motivation to change?"

You also want to make sure your young adult knows that while you won't necessarily solve their money problems, you are there for them to listen and offer advice. But we need to hold back from telling them what to do and instead focus on helping them figure out what they want to do. Tori Dunlap has a big warning for parents to make sure their kids know they will give them the space they need to be financial grownups – and that the parents accept their modified role. "You know your kid better than anybody else, and you know your family and financial situation better than anybody else. Parents of this generation are often very good at gaslighting their own children."

Dunlap encourages parents to help their kids use money as a tool to build the life they want and to focus on the goals and priorities of their kids even if they are different from what the parents had in mind for them. Here is a sample dialogue from her:

"I know that you want to live on your own when you graduate college and you don't want roommates anymore, you know? Okay. Well, that's going to mean that you maybe have to increase your salary or increase your side hustle or decrease your spending. And I know that's really important to you, so how can I help support you in that?"

That is a very different conversation from, "How could you be so stupid and spend a bunch of money on brunch?" Dunlap explains that if parents use that kind of hurtful language, not only will their kids hide their money struggles from them, but it will also damage their overall relationship with their young adult. By framing money discussions around goals that they want, we keep the conversation flowing and our relationship with your young adult children can evolve.

The gift of success is stepping back and letting them become financial grownups. Perhaps when you least expect it, there will come a time when your young adult children will start to proactively ask for your guidance and, yes, even fly on their own.

Celebrate Wins

One of the best text messages I ever received from my stepdaughter said, "I have some finance questions. Can I call you tonight or do you have a lot of work?" In other words, I was no longer having to initiate the conversation. She wanted my advice. Even more shocking: she knew I actually had a life and career of my own and respected the fact that the advice was something I was giving to her – not imposing on her.

It is also important to understand that we don't need our kids to know everything. We need them to know how to think for themselves, problem-solve, and know when to reach out for help. As we've learned during the pandemic, we can't be prepared for everything, and we can't expect our kids to be either. But we do have to get them to that aha moment where they realize that, yes, they are fully capable of being financial grownups.

Jean Chatzky, CEO of HerMoney.com, remembers seeing that light bulb come on for her young adult children as they started earning money. "They realized the value of an hour of their time. Any money that they earn was always far more valuable to them than any money that they got for an allowance or for a birthday. I think that's because they've got skin in the game, but it also made them think differently about how they were going to use that money." Chatzky says her kids were much more deliberate about what was worth it once they were earning money and could calculate that it took x hours of time to buy something. "All of a sudden they thought about it more carefully. "

Mandi Siegel Zucker, one of the many parents I connected with on the Grown and Flown Parents Facebook page, shared her win:

When my oldest son was applying for college, he really wanted a big, public state school. When we got all his financial aid and scholarship money, a small, private school without D1 sports or fraternities was much cheaper. I told him he can go wherever he wanted. He came to me and said, "Mom, I'm going to college to study business. And I think the best business decision would be to go to the school that will allow me to get a good education, good job, graduate without debt, and start my life right."

Fast-forward, and her son is now a junior double majoring in finance and accounting. He is living in an apartment and doesn't have a meal plan, so now he has to move into a new phase of adulting where he is responsible for buying his own food. Her son had asked for a good budget, but the question for Mandi was how to even know what the right amount of money was?

Based on how well he had been adapting to college and his interest in being mindful of how much of his parents' money he spent, Mandi took the risk of telling her son to just buy food on the credit card for the first month. But her son decided that rather than just spend without any guardrails, he would take a data-driven look at his past food spending. "He asked how much the meal plan cost last year [$3,400/semester]," Mandi told me.

"He then figured out that it is about $215/week and decided by himself that he wants to spend about half of that on food this semester. Yesterday he called me from the grocery store and said he's buying powdered Gatorade because it's cheaper. Cracked me up because he never would let me buy that at home!"

What's Your Financial Grownup Story?

I've shared many personal experiences throughout this book, and I hope it inspired you to think back to your own experiences learning about money from your parents and maybe your grandparents. For some of us, we were fortunate that our parents purposefully spoke to us about money, and we felt well-prepared going into adult life. For some of us, our lessons came from observing the role money played in our parents' life.

I remember vividly those scheduled budget and later investing meetings with my father where my siblings and I each had a turn having his focused attention. We would discuss our financial needs and plans for the coming semester in college. I also remember tuning him out when he tried to talk me into a career on Wall Street and not in journalism. I wonder now: was he totally frustrated with his headstrong daughter who didn't understand what life would cost?

We learn so much of our consumer behavior during time spent going about the normal day-to-day errands with our parents. I remember going to outlet malls with my mother. There was clearly something in her past that caused her to stockpile goods for fear that they might never be available again. I still have umbrellas from one of these occasions. They were flowered umbrellas at a London Fog outlet in Vermont. She saw them on sale and asked how many there were. And then she bought the entire inventory as the clerk stood there in shock. She passed away in 2005. Every time I see one of those umbrellas, I think of my mom, always afraid if she didn't get something now she would miss her chance.

Take some time to think about how your children will look back on their teen years and early to mid-twenties and the lessons you taught them. Think also about what they probably observed just being around you and other family members. Are you happy with that behavior? What would you change now that you have taken in the information in this book?

Cherish the Memories

Money memories start young. Whether it was the tooth fairy, an allowance, money tied to holidays and cultural milestones, or board games like Monopoly that have underlying lessons, money has always been part of the ritual of growing up.

I remember every time my son Harry received money for a birthday, I would go with him to the bank, have him fill out the deposit form, and then pose for a picture with the check and the deposit slip. Then he had to go up to the window on his own, give it to the teller, and pose for a picture with them so Harry could send it to the relative with a thank-you note. Now it's a cute memory, but at the time it was actually much more of a hassle than just depositing the check myself while he was in school or home with a babysitter.

I truly believe that going through the motions does help make it real. And I hope I've been able to help you realize that while we can tell our kids about money and ask them to do money related things, action matters, too. Pushing young adults to be financial grownups, even though we are still watching them and making sure it is done correctly the first few times, is essential.

Although I've put it out there that this book is for parents whose children are 16 to 26 years old, the truth is that the journey of being a parent is forever. Not everything will be done at the time it "should" be. As I shared in the last chapter, not until I was writing this book did it occur to me that my two over-18-year-old kids needed to have an advance directive. I just never thought about it. So I reached out to them, explained it and why it mattered, and we got it done. I procrastinated because I thought I would get a ton of pushback. I didn't! They not only understood it but also were into it. They had very specific ideas about what they wanted, and I was pretty impressed with the logic behind their decisions. I was able to step back and just observe as they filled out the forms and clicked submit. Full disclosure: I still had to stay on top of them for the notary part. I'm guessing very few of their peers are aware of and in possession of living wills and power of attorney documents. I hope this book will boost that number and make it a normal mainstream thing to do when kids turn 18.

Going through this book and then working with your kids on the various steps you need to take as a family to launch them as financial grownups will create incredible memories for your family. In the short term those memories might not be as fun as a family trip to Iceland, but you might be surprised how into it they get once they realize what they will get out of educating themselves about money.

In my case, 21-year-old Brad will proudly share how much his Roth IRA is currently worth. He can also explain his asset allocation and diversification strategy should you ask. We also regularly talk about how he prices and negotiates his work for clients as he grows his content creation business. My 24-year-old, Ashley, beams with pride when asked about what it is like to own your own co-op apartment in New York City at such a young age. And watch out if you dare ask her who pays that mortgage! It's all her, and don't even suggest she is dependent on her parents to help out. We don't contribute – and she likes it that way.

If you've done your job right, stepping back may still be hard for you. But your children will probably surprise you with how ready they are for whatever money decisions come their way. Consider having quarterly family money meetings where you can each discuss how you are investing money and what looks interesting for the future. Have them present their 401(k) or other investing vehicles and share their asset allocation decisions. Ask their opinion about money decisions you might be making. If you have a financial advisor, ask them to add your children to their email list when they send out newsletters, and then discuss the newsletter with your kids.

And be there to listen. Your young adults will know when to come to you and will always be thankful to you for giving them the gift of launching them as financial grownups.

Review

1. Don't be discouraged if your kids aren't listening to you. Work on your messaging.
2. Let them be their own version of financial grownups in a way that reflects their priorities, which may not be the same as yours.
3. Resist "saving them" when they make mistakes, even if there are financial consequences.
4. Be clear with your children that your resources go first to your priorities.
5. Don't judge their financial decisions. Instead create a dialogue to help them come to their own conclusions about the best ways to make their dreams happen.
6. Create and cherish the memories of launching your financial grownups.
7. Always be there to listen and to celebrate their grownup life.

Epilogue

My Advice for Financial Grownups
By Ashley Jessica Kaufman

Money Tips for Young Adults

When I was asked to write the epilogue for my stepmother's book about my best money-saving tips, I was up for the challenge. As you know by reading this book, I am two years out of college and own my first home. Along the way, I have compiled a long list of ways to save money every month, most of which I learned from my parents during childhood.

Compare Prices Across Stores

Growing up, my parents taught me not to just buy something the first place I see it because it is likely cheaper somewhere else. So, while you may want something the moment you see it in that first store, don't give in to instant gratification. Instead, shop around first to ensure you are getting the best price—a process that's been simplified with the ability to look everything up on a cell phone. I've practiced this habit with everything from a cat stuffed animal from the stationary store by my childhood home to the couch I'm writing this on. It's always worth checking somewhere else to see what the price could be for a similar item, or even the same item, at another store.

When I moved into college, everything in my dorm room, my roommates' things included, were purchased at Bed Bath and Beyond or Target, because it was simple, easy, and close to campus. Generally, when shopping at a big box store, many assume the prices are standard across the board, that the stores all price things similarly because they need to compete with each other, or that the prices are set by the manufacturer.

When I moved into my apartment, I decided to put this theory to the test. I made a spreadsheet. I'm a spreadsheet kind of girl: if it can be done in Excel, it will be done in Excel. In this spreadsheet, I had a list of the 150 items that I needed for my apartment: everything from a couch and mattress to a spatula and tongs. Within this spreadsheet, I had my top stores for home essentials listed out – Ikea, Bed Bath and Beyond, Target, Walmart, and Amazon – and there I went through and wrote out the different prices for each of these 150 items at each of these five stores. Some specialty items had to come from a different store, but almost everything came from one of those five. What I found was the stores that you assume are the cheapest likely aren't for every item. A shower curtain might be $5 from Amazon yet the rings to attach it cost $8—but are only $1 at Walmart. So I had to mix and match where everything came from. My friends told me I was crazy for this and that I was "inconveniencing myself over $2," but I ended up saving around $500 in the end, which I was able to spend on something else I had really wanted and previously did not have room in my budget for before: an espresso machine.

When making final decisions on what to buy, there were a few items where I picked a more expensive option, like purchasing All Clad cookware instead of a brand on Amazon I had never heard of. I wanted to consider the quality of the item because, chances are, a good set of pots and pans will last me much longer than something random I bought because it was cheap.

Another thing to consider is price matching. Many large chain stores and some smaller stores will price match if you find the exact same item cheaper somewhere else and can show it to them. My father taught me this lesson about 10 years ago when I got my first iPhone. The Otterbox case that would keep that new and shiny phone safe was around $40 at Best Buy. While we were in the store, he took out his phone and pulled up the same case at another store, which was selling for $30. Best Buy was happy to match that price because they were still getting a sale.

Split Up Costs with Friends

Since high school, through college, and even now my friends and I have been splitting the cost of things to save a few dollars. In high school, it was things like buying the large bag of chips and sharing it instead of getting individual ones (this was before COVID-19), which would end up saving us around $2–3 every day before musical rehearsal. In college, it was sharing Ubers to get to our friend's apartment when the bus was not an option or convincing more people to join in on sorority merchandise purchases so we could buy in bulk and get a lower rate per item.

Now as an adult, we save by sharing things like streaming subscriptions and Costco memberships. Some of my friends even have family phone plans with other friends. I also share streaming subscriptions with my parents. Recently, I contributed to the "family ecosystem," as my stepmother calls it, by subscribing to Showtime and Paramount+, which my entire family is welcome to use just as I use their subscriptions. Whether it's with friends or with my family, there are always small ways to save just a few dollars, which can be invested or saved to buy things, like an apartment.

Consider the Long Term

As I discussed before, sometimes quality outweighs the cost of an item and will save you money in the long run. When I purchased my espresso machine, I did my research and bought the best machine I could afford. Are there much cheaper options on Amazon? Yes, but I realized that if I bought the nicer machine I could eventually upgrade it with easy-to-install, do-it-yourself upgrades that wouldn't break the bank. Plus, the coffee coming out of it would also taste leaps and bounds better than the coffee from the inexpensive machine. I've used this logic throughout many of my purchases in the past few years.

Growing up, my family and I went to Walt Disney World many times, took a trip to Disneyland at some point, and even went on a Disney Cruise. Since my first trip to Disney in 1998, I've been hooked on everything relating to theme parks. I had always heard of these annual pass programs at theme parks and amusement parks everywhere we went. Busch Gardens, Six Flags, even Playland in Rye, New York—they all have annual or season pass programs. When I was growing up, my family never lived close enough to one of these places to warrant having an annual pass. As an adult, though, I hold a Walt Disney World annual pass—yes, to a theme park located in Florida, which I, living in Manhattan, think is worth it.

In 2020, before the pandemic hit, my boyfriend and I were planning a trip to Walt Disney World in Florida. He's a massive Star Wars fan, and when we were last there in October 2019 for a few days, the new Star Wars ride was still under construction. So as we were planning our 2020 trip and pricing out this vacation, the cost of everything was weighing on us. We were not even a year out of college, and dropping $2,000 to go on vacation for a few days seemed excessive. After doing some research, I learned about Disney's annual pass program. It seemed excessive to spend so much money on park tickets for just one trip, so I made a spreadsheet. Disney's platinum annual passes—the only option for people who do not live in Florida—include a 20% discount on merchandise and snacks sold in gift shops, a 10% discount on food, park entry with no blackout dates, photos taken in the parks (which are way better quality than I would take on my phone), and hotel discounts. When I broke everything down into what one day at Disney costs—cost of entrance plus what we spend in a day including food and hotels—it was easy to see whether this would be worth it for us or not.

Ultimately, we decided that if we used the pass for two four- to five-day trips per year, we would break even. So we took the plunge and said that we'd do one year and then reevaluate. After all our discounts and maximizing our discount options, the pass paid for itself in one trip. We just renewed this pass because of everything that's come with it, and we're looking to go to Hawaii next year, something previously out of my price point, because the Disney annual pass also comes with seasonal discounts for Aulani, the Disney resort in Hawaii.

Discounts

I've been able to leverage a variety of discounts through the company I work for and using my brother's perks at NYU. My brother purchased new sneakers for me with his discount. Of course I paid him back, but it was 20% off what I would have paid if I purchased them on my own. I recommend always looking for a discount code, whether offered through student discount programs, corporate programs, or a browser extension that checks for discount codes online. They're out there for nearly every website.

Those annoying pop-ups you get when you visit a website? Yeah, usually those are offering 5–30% off purchases for new subscribers to a newsletter. You can always unsubscribe, but for the purchase you're going to make online, it's worth the sign-up.

Additionally, this is a tip my stepmother, Bobbi, told me about. If you have an account on a particular website, and you are logged in, if you add something you're looking at to your cart and then navigate off the website, many websites will send you a discount code to your email within the next 24-48 hours. By having the patience to wait for the code to arrive, you can save hundreds of dollars, depending on the purchase.

Discounts are everywhere, for everything: you just need to look and have some patience. Sometimes things will go on sale days after you buy them and you need to think it over; that's also an option.

Maximize Credit Card Offers and Join Loyalty Programs

I'm sure at some point you've gotten a letter in the mail about a great card you're prequalified for, or you've surfed NerdWallet to learn about which credit card is right for you. My biggest money-saving tip comes from learning to maximize credit card sign-on bonuses and offers. I have three credit cards, and I think it's important to make an informed decision and pick the card that works for you while maximizing the sign-on bonus.

When you visit a website, it creates cookies—little crumbs left behind that you had been there before. It's how targeted ads are pushed to you: they suggest what they think you'll like based on your internet search activity. Once you've picked out a card, close the tab. Chances are within a couple of days you'll get an advertisement pushed to you for a card with a better sign-on bonus with more points offered. If not, try a private browsing session, and something better is likely to pop up with some patience.

This method alone helped me get 75,000 American Express points when I spent the minimum required for the Gold card sign-on bonus. It is important to note, however, that cards with better point values and better redemption options will likely cost a yearly fee. Some cards with no annual fee have decent point multiplier options and redemption values, but this is important to research and find what works for you.

In 2019 I decided that in 2022 I'd go on a trip to Japan. The pandemic happened and messed up that entire timeline, but I am at a point where between all of my points and loyalty programs, I have a combined 500,000 points and could fund my entire dream trip to Tokyo without spending a dime on fancy hotels and business class flights. Though my trip will be delayed by COVID-19, I'm excited and ready to go when that time does come around.

While not all points are made equally, joining loyalty programs and sticking with the companies you pick is the easiest way to save money in the long run. Before picking a program, I'd recommend searching around and looking for the best option for what you're looking for, longer-term, not just the most convenient at that moment in time.

Throughout my childhood, my father traveled for work, and we would always go on nice vacations and go to fun and exciting new places, but it was because he had saved all of these points. For my college graduation, my father took us to Atlantis to celebrate. This beautiful hotel in the Bahamas was completely paid for with points, and that realization sparked my interest in banking points.

Buy Refurbished

Electronics should always be researched before they are purchased. I'm writing this on a 2015 MacBook that has lasted me this long because I did the research and purchased a device that would last the test of time. When purchasing electronics or small kitchen appliances, the term *refurbished* comes up a lot, and it's hard to determine whether buying refurbished electronics are worth it.

Oftentimes, refurbished electronics cost significantly less than their brand-new counterparts; however, it is important to purchase these devices from either licensed repair shops, the original manufacturer, or another trusted source. Refurbished electronics usually contain pieces and parts from an old machine or computer to build a new product. Refurbished goods also usually have a shorter warranty than new products, so that is definitely something to look out for. However, refurbished goods often undergo much more extensive testing to ensure they work than new products do, so you're likely to get a device that functions the same or potentially better than a brand-new item.

* * *

While these tips may not apply to everyone, as a 25-year-old with a mortgage, two years out of college, this is how I've pulled together the money needed for a down payment. Every dollar that I've saved from these methods has been extremely helpful to achieve my own goals and get to where I currently am, and they'll continue to help me grow. I hope you've found them useful.

Ashley Kaufman

Notes

Introduction

1. https://mlaem.fs.ml.com/content/dam/ml/registration/ml_parentstudy-brochure.pdf
2. https://www.55places.com/blog/survey-reveals-empty-nesters-still-supporting-children-financially

Chapter 1

1. https://www.smh.com.au/education/profoundly-dangerous-a-generation-at-risk-from-concierge-parents-20190322-p516q0.html

Chapter 2

1. https://www.bankrate.com/pdfs/pr/20190424-financial-independence-survey.pdf
2. https://www.creditcards.com/credit-card-news/pay-adult-childrens-debt-poll/

Chapter 3

1. https://dweb.news/2021/07/12/parents-hand-over-nearly-gbp3000-a-year-to-their-grown-up-children-to-help-pay-for-food-cover-household-bills-fund-holidays-or-even-aid-first-home-purchases/
2. Ibid.
3. https://www.urban.org/sites/default/files/publication/100106/reshaping_parent_plus_loans.pdf
4. https://www.nerdwallet.com/article/loans/student-loans/whats-the-average-parent-plus-loan-debt

Chapter 4

1. https://www.teenvogue.com/story/gina-rodriguez-student-loans/
2. https://www.usnews.com/education/best-colleges/paying-for-college/articles/paying-for-college-infographic
3. https://www.yahoo.com/now/parent-plus-loans-much-debt-182311002.html#:~:text=According%20to%202021%20federal%20College,the%20onset%20of%20the%20pandemic.
4. https://www.elle.com/uk/life-and-culture/news/g30191/emma-watsons-best-quotes-of-all-time/

Chapter 7

1. https://www.pewresearch.org/internet/2021/04/07/social-media-use-in-2021/
2. https://influencermarketinghub.com/influencer-marketing-2019-benchmark-report/
3. https://nrf.com/blog/how-brands-can-use-social-connect-gen-z

Chapter 8

1. https://www.ebri.org/docs/default-source/ebri-issue-brief/ebri_ib_538_hsalong-16sep21.pdf?sfvrsn=f2673b2f_4

Chapter 10

1. https://www.freelancersunion.org/insurance/disability/
2. https://www.ifebp.org/bookstore/education-benefits-survey-results/Pages/education-benefits-survey-results-2019.aspx
3. https://buck.com/survey-2020-financial-wellbeing-and-voluntary-benefits-survey/
4. https://shrm.org/ResourcesAndTools/hr-topics/benefits/pages/converting-pto-funds-to-student-loan-relief-is-a-timely-benefit.aspx
5. https://doublethedonation.com/tips/matching-grant-resources/matching-gift-statistics/
6. Ibid.
7. https://naphia.org/industry-data/. https://content.naic.org/cipr_topics/topic_pet_insurance.htm

Chapter 12

1. https://www.morganstanley.com/ideas/us-pets-investing-trend

Acknowledgments

This book would not have been possible without the two financial grownups who served as the inspiration. Thank you to both Ashley and Bradley for stepping up your game to become the role models you are. You are now total rock stars when it comes to advance directives, Roth IRAs, mortgages, taxes, investing, so many insurance products, and more.

Thank you to my fantastic literary agent Sarah Smith and to the team at the David Black Agency, as well as to Kevin Harreld, Susan Cerra, and the team at Wiley.

I am eternally grateful to my talent agent Adam Kirschner for his career advice, advocacy, and friendship.

The heart and soul of this book are the exceptional group of parenting and financial experts: Andy Hill, Allison Task, Anne-Lyse Wealth, Amanda Clayman, Amy Blacklock, Brad Klontz, Catherine Newman, Cynthia Meyer, David Stein, Janine Halloran, Jason Feifer, Jean Chatzky, Julie Lythcott-Haims, Kelly Long, KJ Dell'Antonia, Leslie Tayne, Mary Dell Harrington, Michael Eisenberg, Pam Capalad, Ron Lieber, Roy Feifer, Shawn Rochester, Tonya Rapley, Tori Dunlap, and Vicki Cook.

Thank you to my many friends and colleagues who have patiently listened to my ideas and encouraged and supported me for the many years this book has been in development, including Ashley Wall, Steve Stewart, Joe Saul-Sehy, Erica Keswin, Pam Samuels, Janis Cecil, Jill Kasner, Elizabeth Koraca, Trae Bodge, Laura Rowley, Liz Elting, Caroline Shapiro, Erin Lowry, Allison Weiss Brady, Lindsay Goldwert, Jennifer Barrett, Cari Sommer, Jennifer Owens, Amy Rosenberg, Andrea Woroch, David Bach, Jamila Souffrant, Lauren Smith Brody, Elizabeth Gerst, Melissa McGoff, Jenny Leon, Greg Siers, Brian Dean, Michael Mathis, Caely Hibbits, and Susan McPherson.

For more than two decades I have had the privilege to be part of a very special book club whose members are Erika Greff, Melissa Stoller, Marcy Winkler, Felice Farber, Jenni Singer, Valerie Kerr, and Loryn Bergman. Love you all!

To my friends at MCC: Thank you for the pep talks on the golf course and at the 19th hole and for the word count check-ins.

This book is dedicated to my father and mother, but I am also grateful to have the support of my stepmother Susan Rebell and my in-laws Monica and Ed Kaufman. Thank you also to Deborah Rebell Moss, Jason Moss, Asher Moss, and Sienna Moss as well as to Jon Rebell and Noah Levine.

To my future financial grownup, Harry. You are the love of my life, and while I know you have to be a grownup one day, you will always be my baby boy.

And finally, to my husband and best friend, Neil. Thank you for bragging about me to everyone who will listen, for pushing me to do things I didn't think I was good enough to do, and of course for always doing the night walks with our Morkie, Waffles.

* * *

About the Author

Bobbi Rebell is a financial literacy advocate and a CERTIFIED FINANCIAL PLANNER™ professional. She is a speaker, conference host, and moderator, and works as a spokesperson for brands aligned with her values. Bobbi is also the host of the critically acclaimed *Money Tips for Financial Grownups* podcast, which has more than 700,000 downloads. In 2021 she launched a new venture, GrownupGear.com, as a fun way to promote adulting and being a financial grownup. Earlier in her career Bobbi was a global business news anchor and personal finance columnist at Reuters and held various journalist positions at top news outlets including CNBC, CNN, and PBS. Bobbi is a graduate of the University of Pennsylvania and received her Certificate in Financial Planning from New York University. Her first book *How to Be a Financial Grownup: Proven Advice from High Achievers on How to Live Your Dreams and Have Financial Freedom* was released in 2016. She lives in New York City with her family.

Index